TRUTH

PERSONAS, NEEDS, AND FLAWS IN THE ART OF BUILDING ACTORS AND CREATING CHARACTERS

SUSAN BATSON

DEDICATION

TO MY TWO GREATEST TEACHERS.

Ruth Batson, my mother, taught me that life's task is the betterment of the human condition.

Carl Ford, my son, continues to teach me unconditional love, self-worth, and the power of dreams.

Their unrelenting commitment to truth and to freedom motivates me every day.

CONTENTS

PART III: THE CHARACTER

PART IV: THE SCRIPT

PART V: THE LIFE

ACKNOWLEDGEMENTS

A SPECIAL acknowledgement to my sister Dorothy Batson Owusu. I started writing a book on a yellow legal pad in 1990, and it was Dorothy who typed what I wrote into her computer. She reminded me of that first attempt and encouraged me to continue.

I wish to pay homage to Bruce Bennett, who met with me regularly in my tragic flaw and coached, coaxed, and conned me into trusting his much-needed skill and insight in the creation of this book. It is his tenacious commitment to the details and the history of acting that has made *Truth* a far better exploration of the art form than I could have produced on my own.

I also wish to thank my publisher, Web Stone, who came to me not for movie star gossip, but for what I understood about acting.

My deepest gratitude to Nicole Kidman and Juliette Binoche. Their contributions have enhanced this book, and their friendship and brilliance have enriched my life.

There would be no book, and no Susan Batson Studio without the vision and leadership of my son, Carl Ford, and the loyalty, dedication, strength, intelligence, and deep kindness of Greg Braun. I am also grateful to the Batson Studio teachers in New York—Francesca Harper, Fred Waggoner, James Lee, Luca Manganaro, Marion Cantone, Nina Binder, Sebastian Galvez, Tina Alexis Allen, Tom Brangle, and Wass Stevens.

A very special thanks to Mary Setrakian for giving the Studio the best musical department in theater.

My gratitude to all the actors (students and professionals) who have entrusted me with their precious gifts.

I must acknowledge the mentorship of the great teachers who taught me. Herbert Berghof taught me that acting is a Primary Art Form with a responsibility to humanity. Uta Hagen was a tough taskmaster who stripped me of my bullshit. Lee Strasberg led me to the intimacy that is the heart of acting for me, and gave my talent his blessing. Harold Clurman embraced my abilities and gave me the priceless gift of responsibility to the text.

Many thanks also to those great educators who encouraged me as a young amateur—Lewis, Adele Thane, Leo Nickole, Richard E. Arnold, and Paul J. Austin.

INTRODUCTION

AN ACTOR'S life, like any artist's life, is a long, long road. But an actor doesn't walk that road alone. Acting is collaborative. It's always a group effort. If you're lucky, along the way you meet someone with whom your collaboration becomes so vital and so rich that the two of you naturally fall into step together. For me, Susan Batson is that Person.

This book you hold is called *Truth*, and that title precisely describes the core of the work Susan and I do together. I can't create unless I have truth—I have to feel it. Susan helps me to find the truth in myself and use its purity, intimacy, and honesty to make my work real. She's helped me to nurture and protect truth in myself and in the characters that I've played. What I've learned from Susan is how to keep the truth alive no matter what.

There's a beautiful mystery to acting. That mystery is irresistible to me. Every actor has his or her own feelings on this subject; but personally I see myself as a conduit. When you're acting you are a vessel—there is something beyond you that is working through you. It's not about who you are. It's not about your ego. Truthful acting is about being available and open and offering up your deepest, darkest secrets and saying, "Here they are." It's about creating and morphing and changing. Anything in me or around me can wind up in the work, as long as it is *true*.

I first met Susan in New York just a week before I made *Peacemaker*. We worked together in earnest for two years on *Eyes Wide Shut* in London and on every film I've done since, wherever they've taken us. An actor's work doesn't end after any one particular project; and the journey Susan and I have shared over the last twelve years has never been solely focused on one particular achievement. There's so much more to acting than just creative success. It runs thicker and deeper than that. It has to— it's in my blood, it beats through me. I know that it's in Susan's blood, too. I feel like we've been together my whole life.

In our work together, Susan has seen all my different places and identities. She has known me as a daughter, a mother, a sister, and a wife. More than anybody in my life, Susan has access to my encyclopedia of emotions. We literally have and share words that trigger sensations in me and in the characters I play. It's a beautiful, guiding, intuitive, and very smart person that can make that happen. Susan combines a powerful intellect with a powerful emotional life. She's as intuitive as she is intelligent. Both those sides of her are very well balanced. I try to maintain that same balance, both in my life and in my work.

We all have our protective shells. Things happen in your life that encourage you to break the shell down, and other things happen that make you build that shell back up again. This is particularly true on the sometimes quite demoralizing and sometimes quite extraordinary artistic road down which Susan and I travel. My time with Susan has taught me to work with my shell. Her collaboration has made me so much more confident as an actor We all have our protective shells. Things happen in your life that encourage you to break the shell down, and other things happen that make you build that shell back up again. This is particularly true on the sometimes quite demoralizing and sometimes quite extraordinary artistic road down which Susan and I travel. My time with Susan has taught me to work with my shell. Her collaboration has made me so much more confident as an actor; and her friendship has made me more confident as a woman. No matter what has come, I've never crumbled. Susan won't let me.

A great teacher can make anything seem possible. So many of the actors I've admired and idolized and, in a few lucky instances, been blessed to work with, were shaped and inspired by teachers who opened them to the possibilities of their art. Among actors, Lee Strasberg, Sanford Meisner, and Jeff Corey are just as legendary as their pupils Marilyn Monroe, Robert Duvall, and Jack Nicholson. I am confident that Susan Batson will go down in history as one of acting's legendary teachers. I only hope that my work can contribute to her legend.

Susan signs her letters "Always in the Art." Susan and I will travel side by side for the rest of my actor's journey. We'll be "always in the art" together, and I'll always be grateful that I found her.

And now, through this book, you've found her, too.

—Nicole Kidman,

January 2006

PROLOGUE

Greatest truth fire cannot burn nor water drown it.
Alexander Dumas, *The Count of Monte Cristo*

The way to truth by the minute examinations of facts,
that is the way of scientist. A hard and thankless way. It's
not the way of the poet. He apprehends truth by power:
the truth which he apprehends cannot be defined save by
greater power, and there is no greater power.
John Masefield, *Shakespeare and the Spiritual Life*

THE RIDE

I live on the Upper West Side of Manhattan. Every day, a driver named Segundo picks me up and takes me to the acting studio that my son and I founded in the theater district. Since I'm always either cloistered at home reading scripts, or holed up working until all hours at the studio, I've come to love my transitional trips downtown. I look forward to turning onto the West Side Highway and putting the city to one side for a while. Even though I'm usually talking on my cell phone most of the way, I gaze out the car window at the water, and I am reminded that there is a deep, flowing universe of ideas and people to explore.

A few blocks before we turn onto Forty-Fourth Street, there's a billboard promising a *Continuous Show of Live Nude Girls* on *Two Stages*. This always yanks me back into reality. Some of the actors I work with dance in that club or others like it in New York and New Jersey. For me, it's a daily reality check of the kinds of choices actors make to stay alive.

Segundo pulls up at the door to my studio. In a few steps, I'm through the door, inside the studio's office, and going over the day's schedule with my staff. Everyone who works for me is an actor. Some of them barter their time working in my office for my time working with them in class. I've never regretted this arrangement. They've made the same commitment that I have: not just to show up, but also to arrive prepared and ready to work. That is what I believe in. That is what I'm all about—*doing the work.*

And that also goes for my first class today. It's open to all, regardless of experience. Anyone who walks in off the street with a desire to work and a passion to create is welcome. An open class like this one helps me to determine what level the actors are on, and how we at the Studio can best serve them. It also gives the actors an opportunity to get a sense of who I am and what my process is. They have to see if my studio is the right place for them. It has also proven to be the best way to get rid of the imposters who don't want to do the work!

When I enter the studio, since I'm in a world I've been in since I was eight years old, it's the only place I ever feel really comfortable. I love sharing this demanding and miraculous art form of acting. It's in this spirit that we get down to work.

PART

I

THE *NEED*, *PUBLIC PERSONA*, AND *TRAGIC FLAW*

CHAPTER ONE

THE CIRCLE

Our social personality is the creation of others.
Marcel Proust

THE CLASS

My finger hits play on a portable CD player and Curtis Mayfield sings:

People get ready, there's a train a coming

I raise my voice above the music—

"I will call each of you into the center of the circle, one by one, to move with the music. You can express yourself in whatever way you want. The rest of you remain on the outside of the circle and follow the person in the center. Surrender to each person's imagination, to that person's sexuality, sense of rhythm and emotional experience—and character! Open yourself up to that person's sense of self!"

"All right, a new character is entering the center of the circle!"

You don't need no baggage, you just get on board.

Drew Winslett

Drew can't wait to take the circle. On her way into the center, she peels off her sweater like a stripper. She's all impulse with no brakes—potentially a great talent.

She feels the heat that she's bringing to the rest of the class, and enjoys everyone moving with her. The actors on the outside of the circle are looking, moving, and giving 100 percent. Drew finds this attention thrilling.

But as confident as she seems, what this girl is really doing is people-pleasing—operating from the responses of others more than trusting her own instincts. The only inner voice she's listening to is the one doubting herself—pushing her to give more and more and more until she's beyond the reach of her own self-respect.

All you need is faith to hear the diesels humming
You don't need no ticket, you just thank the Lord

"A new character has taken the center. Open yourselves up to him!"

Eastwood De Wayne

Before he took the center of the circle, this handsome, confident he-man did a disco step while staring down every person in the room. I chuckled, glad that he could make fun of himself. But once he's in the center, self-consciousness seizes his body and lets him know what truly rules him. He transforms into a stiff-legged stud. In the outer circle, everyone stiffens along with him, forcing him to face a circular mirror vision of his vulnerability.

All the weakness and anxiety that this guy has trained himself to hide is coming out into the open. The hidden fear he's exposing has driven him to put on a tough façade; but that fear probably also drove him to my class. I know that on the other side of that fear is the courage to create.

There is something wonderfully fragile about self-consciousness, like the blush on a tough guy's cheek. As I watch Eastwood struggle to stay a stud, I hope he'll get to know the poet in him.

Faith is the key. open the doors and board them
There's hope for all among those loved the most

"*Another new character!*"

Sean Dean

Brooding, dark, somber—as part of the outer circle he barely moved. He wouldn't try dropping in—opening himself up—to anyone else's character and personality. But when he's called to the center, Sean clenches his fists, his face contorts, and he sinks to his knees. Tears stream down his cheeks as he claws at the floor. His emotional depth is intense. But he'll have to learn that acting is not emoting, it's DOING. He has to become invested in what makes a character a walking, talking human being, not in his own histrionics. His powerful emotional life is a natural gift. If used well, that gift could make him a great actor.

There ain't no room for the hopeless sinner
Who would hurt all mankind just to save his own

"And another one! Come to the center!"

Angelina La Monroe

Sleek, curvy, she oozes sex as she slinks into the circle. But her eyes tell a different story than her body. That gaze, smoldering from below her heavy eyelids, tells me that this beauty aches for approval. She covers that ache with ambition. And that ambition is what has made her the supermodel she is today. I'm moved by her need for approval. Angelina knows she can turn heads, but I don't think she knows she can do what very few actors can do—really touch people.

Have pity on those whose chances grow thinner,
For there is no hiding place against the kingdom's throne

"Come on, get ready!"

Peter Von Sellers

As each person took the center of the circle, Peter perfectly mimicked that person's movements with devastating accuracy. Alone in the center, he incorporates moves from everyone else who has come before him. Peter's a natural impressionist and knows exactly what quirky and distinctive element of each person to spin into that person's caricature. He even has the nerve to do *me*—and I roar with laughter! But I do question whether his impressionist is willing to allow us to see *him*. In order to breathe life into a character, he's going to have to find, reveal, and use exactly who he *is*.

People get ready, there's a train a coming
You don't need no baggage, you just get on board

"Here comes a new character!"

<u>Brigitte Berry</u>

Lean, expressionless, dressed in sweat clothes—as soon as the music started, Brigitte began to move expertly and powerfully. Inside the circle, the girl is unstoppable. Her motions are so strong and graceful that they're impossible for the rest of the circle to follow. Dancer, athlete, martial artist—whatever she is, she's got control, discipline, and moves galore. The uncountable hours she's spent at the barre or in the gym have paid off.

Brigitte's commitment to her body's capabilities is admirable. But her movement lacks soul. I'm guessing that there is an emotional volcano waiting to erupt underneath her perfectly controlled and sculpted exterior.

All you need is faith to hear the diesels humming
You don't need no ticket, you just thank the Lord

"One more! Stay focused!"

Harrison Costner

A tall, white-bread Midwesterner, he could be a cowboy or a Kennedy. Harrison seems intimidated by the people like Dean, who gushed tears when they took their turns in the center. Inside the circle himself, he just complies with my instructions, opening up enough that his sexuality and sense of humor come out and nothing more.

Outside the circle, he's shocked by strong emotional displays. Inside the circle, he's safely zipped up in his own charm. Those are two red flags. I can catch glimpses of a complex psyche— flickers of anger and hurt—underneath his buttoned-down facade. I see my task as giving him permission to let the "guy" melt away and let his authentic self express itself.

THE HIT

Curtis sings, the actors move in and out of the circle, and I get a hit—a feeling—a clear intuition about each of the people in my class. I'm *dropping in* to each Person, into the energy of personality and the sensations of each individual's life experience coming from the center of that circle. I'm fascinated by these actors' defenses. And I'm encouraged by the strength and truth of what they're willing to show.

Twenty-four hours a day, seven days a week, we are walking and talking in a character. It's a character we've unconsciously and consciously developed over a lifetime. Model, waiter, writer, carpenter, attorney, plastic surgeon, housewife, corporate exec—

we all behave in ways that define the character we've created for ourselves as we've grown up from infancy into our adult lives.

In the circle together, these actors share the ins and outs of the traps of their given characters. They also show me just how willing they are to let go of their own character and drop into another character. The ability to step into another person's essence is an integral part of the art form of acting.

Acting is a craft—a disciplined art form that uses everything that makes an individual artist unique—from the DNA up. When you can find the joy of using the good, the bad, the ugly, the evil, and the sublime in yourself to create a scripted character, you're on your way to expertly practicing this craft. The more you're willing to share the events and sensations that have made you who you are, the better an artist you will be. The more willing you are to tell the truth, the stronger an actor you will be.

Acting is not therapy. It's personally enlightening, but it's not therapy. In fact, a lot of what I encourage actors to do, a therapist would forbid. A therapist asks you to change, control, or modify your behavior. I tell you to USE IT! Acting demands that you celebrate the wild, the sinful, or the painful places within you. Use your imagination to expose and lift what's already inside you into art.

Passionately applying yourself to the craft of acting on a daily basis is a never-ending responsibility. If you cannot uphold this responsibility—if your artistic will, desire, courage, or strength of character does not enable you to follow through—go back to Peoria! You're not in the right art form! And for sure, my process is not right for you.

TRUTH

Fictional characters didn't spring to life fully formed at the beginning of their stories any more than actors do when they arrive in class. It's the old wounds, the deep fears, the sacred hopes, the deeds, and the circumstances of our lives that reveal who we are. Actors investigate all these things—in themselves and in the characters they play. An actor's investigation looks into the substance of what makes us the human beings we are.

Every scripted character has three basic dimensions—*Public Persona*, *Need*, and *Tragic Flaw*. Every person has the same three dimensions. In order to really act—to breathe life into a script—you must identify and explore these dimensions in yourself.

CHAPTER TWO

THE FACE

And pomp, and feast, and revelry,
With mask, and antique pageantry,
Such sights as youthful poets dream
On summer eves by haunted stream.
John Milton, *"L'Allegro"*

THE STORY

Acting is as old as the Stone Age. When members of a hunter-gatherer tribe formed a circle around a fire and told the stories of their daily struggles and conquests, they were the first actors.

Time passed, civilizations developed, and the circle grew. The fire went out, but the shape remained. That circle became a great half-circle of stone seats carved into the side of a hill—the Classical Greek theater.

Actors uphold a great tradition. We are craftspeople who create true life out of words. That tradition has its roots in the Stone Age, but was reborn in ancient Greece. We actors are the children of Thespis of Icarus—the actor who reinvented our centuries-old human ritual as a modern art.

THE MASK

In the fifth century BC, the Greeks were at a storytelling crossroads.

Up to that time, their communication rituals had been split into two separate camps. In one camp were the epic poets—the "goat singers"—who traveled from city to city, entertaining crowds with solo recitations of long story-poems that were part of their life's work to memorize. These epic poets communicated their stories in the third person. They didn't give voices to the heroes of their stories, or lend their own faces to them; they only described their heroes' journeys, and commented on their fates.

In another camp was the "dithyramb": a kind of ceremonial poem performed in the theater at the Dionysian revels each spring. Part sacred ceremony, part exuberant celebration, and part ritualistic "magic," the dithyramb combined the primitive with the formal. Its fifty performers collectively used their voices and bodies to tell a story as a group, not as individuals. Together, this "chorus" stood in for the will of the gods or for a single character bound to the gods' whims. The entire chorus of anonymous performers danced and sang the roles of individual gods and mortals in unison from behind identical masks.

In search of a more intimate way to communicate with his audience than either of these story rituals offered, a poet and performer named Thespis combined the two. From the epic poets, Thespis took the individual responsibility for telling the story. From the Dionysian chorus, he took the first-person voice, the mask, and the movement. For some long-forgotten ancient religious festival, Thespis painted his face with a bright white lead pigment that distinguished him from the rest of the chorus, took center stage on his own, and interacted in a first-person voice directly with the group chorus.

Thespis fused the individual presentation of the epic poem with the group personification of the dithyramb chorus. By using the face and voice of a single person, Thespis engaged his audience more directly than any epic poet's display of memorized storytelling ever could. When Thespis stepped out from the chorus, he became something more real to his audience than the chorus's symbolic group identity. Thespis had become a character. And his willingness to let his own individuality breathe life from underneath that painted mask distinguished him as the first recognized actor. He is the legendary innovator credited with creating modern drama.

Taking their cue from Thespis's white makeup, his fellow Thespians, as the first actors were then called, began creating masks to transform themselves into the individual characters that this new form of communication demanded. A Greek actor's mask was called a persona. The persona let audiences see inside a character's head and heart through the expressions sculpted into the actor's mask. And as this newly created art of theater grew, the actors' masks also grew in complexity and variety.

Though masks and other theatrical conventions have come and gone, the term *persona* is still with us. Freud's disciple Carl Jung borrowed the Greek word for the actor's mask to describe the masks of personality human beings wear throughout their lives. Jung's *persona* is the face we present to society that covers our true self. Jung believed that every human being creates and maintains a *persona*, a mask we wear that shows the face we'll let the world see.

It's in our faces, in the way we talk, in the way we move. You have a *persona*. Your parents have *personas*; your brothers, sisters, neighbors, and the video store clerk all have *personas*. We all have a face we wear out in public that covers our private self. The same thing is true of scripted characters. A character's innermost thoughts, emotions, and dreams lie just beneath the surface of the mask that that character wears. It's the character's *Public Persona*.

A character's *Public Persona*, like Jung's *persona* and Thespis's mask, is the outer layer of identity that that character offers the rest of the world in the story. For a character, the *Public Persona* is only the first dimension.

CHAPTER THREE

THE
PUBLIC PERSONA

In order to become whole we must try, in a long process, to discover our own personal truth, a truth that may cause pain before giving us a new sphere of freedom.
Alice Miller, *The Drama of the Gifted Child*

THE GANGSTER

Even if we're never shown a moment of a character's childhood or hear a word of dialogue about it, in a story, as in life, adult character grows from the seeds of childhood experience. A character doesn't hatch when it appears on-screen any more than a person's does when we first shake hands with the person.

Whether we're conscious of it or not, the personal obstacles, lingering hurts, and unresolved issues that we experience in childhood remain with us throughout our lives. This pain, this unresolved conflict and unfulfilled desire, unconsciously motivates us to do the things we do and to make the choices that we make. We create a *Public Persona* to hide these vulnerabilities and weaknesses, and all they represent. It's no different for a character in a script.

In *Pulp Fiction*, Vincent Vega drives around Los Angeles bullshitting with his partner Jules and emptying his gun into anyone his gangster-boss orders. Vincent is the perfect guy for his job because he doesn't empathize with the people unlucky enough to wind up in his gun sights. It's easy for Vincent to hurt people when he doesn't experience their pain on an emotional level.

But after the two killers come through a hail of bullets without a scratch, Jules, for one, starts to feel more than he'd like to. As *Pulp Fiction*'s random coincidences pile up, Jules (along with the audience) begins to experience what he and Vincent put their victims through. Jules empathizes and grows. Vincent does not.

Vincent's *Public Persona* is "to be a killer"—a conscienceless gun for hire. But his tough-guy insistence on talking nonstop banalities and doing drugs to numb himself suggests that he has something to hide. His *Public Persona* ("to be a killer") is only a cover concealing a deeper vulnerability. It's only the outside layer of Vincent's character.

Like the mighty Wizard of Oz, Vincent's *Public Persona* says, "Pay no attention to the man behind the curtain." And like the Wizard of Oz, there's a smaller man/child at work pushing buttons behind the *Public Persona* of any character. There's a hidden, insistent, constantly pulsing force from childhood that Vincent's Public Persona covers—his *Need*. Vincent's *Need* is "to be safe."

The *Public Persona* allows us to hide the intimate force of childhood *Need* from the rest of the world. Without the *Public Persona*, we would be helpless against a world that requires the appearance of sanity and stability from infancy on. Imagine Vincent Vega going through *Pulp Fiction* asking everyone he meets to make him feel safe. Absurd? Of course. Yet, it is *Need* that drives Vincent through his life and the story of *Pulp Fiction*, even though he's not even conscious of it. His *Public Persona*, "to be a killer," has grown over his unfulfilled *Need* "to be safe" like a scar grows over a wound.

Great acting moves beneath the mask of *Public Persona*. It reveals and communicates the intimacy that lives underneath the cover—the *Need*. Even though they may not know it, all the people sitting in an audience have a *Public Persona* of their own, and the *Need* it covers. They can sense these two forces at work in a character even if they can't name them. Therefore, to make a character more than one-dimensional, the actor has to know the *Need* that makes the character's covering *Public Persona* necessary.

CHAPTER FOUR

THE *NEED*

Our dreams are made up of yearnings and needs unfulfilled.
Sidney Poitier

"TOMORROW'S ANOTHER DAY"

Once upon a time, in a mythical antebellum South, there lived a rich plantation owner's spoiled daughter named Scarlett O'Hara. But spoiled is only the beginning; for over the course of *Gone With the Wind*, Scarlett schemes, lies, and dupes everyone who makes the mistake of caring about her.

Scarlett is the heroine of the most famous Hollywood movie ever produced. But heroic she is not. This woman is a "dear friend" willing to break up her cousin's marriage, a daughter who acknowledges her father's generosity and sacrifices only after he has lost his mind, and a mother only capable of loving her child after it's dead.

But there's an unfulfilled place inside Scarlett that makes her a schemer, and her manipulations necessary, understandable, even appealing. Scarlett's mask of a manipulating coquette—her *Public Persona*—covers a desire that's as simple as it is powerful.

That desire is her *Need*. Scarlett's Need is a hole within her so deep that if she didn't have her covering *Public Persona* to hide it, she would be helpless. Her *Public Persona* is a coping mechanism. It's a personality that has formed to let her survive in an outside world in which her deeply hidden *Need* remains unfulfilled.

Scarlett's *Need* is "to be protected." She uses her beauty to attract the protective attentions of men. Rhett Butler recognizes that there is a deep *Need* underneath her flirtatious charm and says so: "You should be kissed and kissed often, and by someone who knows how." He knows that Scarlett will only ever feel safe in the arms of a person as obsessed with her as she is with herself.

Every choice Scarlett makes and every scheme that she concocts in *Gone With the Wind*—her pursuit of Ashley, her marriages, her leaving and returning to Tara, her motherhood—is an effort to fulfill that *Need* ("to be protected"). Her *Need* is the single, simple, and primal force that makes her *Public Persona* ("to play the Southern belle") necessary. Scarlett's *Need* drives her character through Margaret Mitchell's book and through David O. Selznick's movie. Vivien Leigh—at twenty—six already an immensely skilled actress—fearlessly exposes the deepest dimension of Scarlett's *character*—the *Need* beneath Scarlett's vivid *Public Persona*.

TRUTH

THE TRUTH

Unfulfilled *Need* is the universal truth at the heart of all characters. There's an unfulfilled *Need* "to be somebody" inside arrogant cruelty (Alonzo Harris — *Training Day* — Denzel Washington). There's an unfulfilled *Need* "to be accepted" at the core of a loner's rebellious anarchy (Lisa - *Girl, Interrupted* — Angelina Jolie).

The *Need* dictates a character's *Public Persona*, not the other way around. Since characters are no more conscious of their primal, controlling *Need* than people are, the way to find a character's *Need* is to examine their *Public Persona*. Simply look at their *Public Persona* and consider what the opposite of that *Public Persona* would be. What *Need* would create this *Public Persona*? What is the *Public Persona* hiding?

Howard — The Aviator — Leonardo DiCaprio
Need: "To be mothered"
Public Persona: "To have no limitations"

Leticia — *Monster's Ball* — Halle Berry
Need: "To be loved"
Public Persona: "To push everyone away"

Bob — Lost in Translation — Bill Murray
Need: "To be pure and honorable"
Public Persona: "To be a hustler"

THE JAM-UP

The balance between *Need* and *Public Persona* is a delicate one. The *Need* is relentless in the way it drives a character through a story. When the *Need* outstrips the *Public Persona*, when that unfulfilled *Need* can no longer be denied and jams up against the *Public Persona*, the third dimension of character is revealed—*Tragic Flaw*.

CHAPTER FIVE

THE
TRAGIC FLAW

When weaving a blanket, an Indian woman leaves a flaw in the
weaving of that blanket to let the soul out.
Martha Graham

THE CHAMELEON

Frank Abagnale Jr. is a smart, personable, well-off teenage boy. He's the apple of his entrepreneur father's eye. He's adored by his mother, a beautiful French war bride. But in the first act of *Catch Me if You Can*, Frank Jr. gets a double dose of the awful truth. Dad is under investigation by the IRS. Mom is having an affair. Frank Jr. idolizes his father and is tormented by the truth of his father's dishonesty. He worships his mother and is equally tormented by the truth of her infidelity.

Frank Jr.'s dad isn't a pillar of the community; he's a crook. Frank Jr.'s mom isn't an exotic prize; she's an unfaithful housewife. Once Frank Jr. learns his family is living a lie, he's not sure who he ever really was. Frank's *Need* is "to have his own identity."

Frank impersonates a substitute teacher so successfully that before long he has people believing he's a lawyer, an airline pilot, and a doctor, amongst many other occupations. His *Public Persona* is "to be everybody." But Frank's not his father; he's not the boy his mother loves; he's not a lawyer, a doctor, or any of the things he pretends to be. He's forging checks along with forging identities—he's a pathological liar. That is Frank's *Tragic Flaw*.

With the FBI closing in, his father in the ground, and his mother remarried, Frank hits his *Tragic Flaw*. His *Need* ("to have his own identity") has jammed up against his *Public Persona* ("to be everybody"). The resulting *Tragic Flaw* ("being a pathological liar") has pushed Frank further away from fulfilling his *Need* than he's ever been. Frank's Tragic Flaw catapults him into the climax of *Catch Me if You Can*.

THE VICTIM

At the opening of *Monster*, Aileen Wuornos describes growing up in a trailer-trash hell. Exploited, brutalized, and ostracized from infancy, her unfulfilled *Need* is "to belong." The cover she forms to hide that *Need* is that of an outlaw—a predator. Her *Public Persona* is "to destroy."

When Aileen becomes enchanted by Selby, she begins to change. She gently seduces Selby and appoints herself Selby's protector. But Aileen's murder spree pushes her *Need* ("to belong") harder and harder against her *Public Persona* ("to destroy"). Aileen's *Tragic Flaw* is that she allows herself to become a victim. She's a ruthless multiple murderer; but with her *Tragic Flaw* controlling her, she becomes the target of Selby's capriciousness and, eventually, the criminal justice system.

THE LONER

Anonymous, invisible, and naïve, Travis Bickle's life in *Taxi Driver* is an urban loner's nightmare of—in Travis's own words—"morbid self-attention." But when Travis connects with a straitlaced campaign worker and a teenage prostitute, his unconscious *Need*—"to be seen"—begins to show through his *Public Persona*—"to be invisible."

Betsy, the campaign worker, sees Travis for who he is, "a walking contradiction," and won't go near him. Iris, the teen prostitute, accepts him for who he is, but offers herself to him as if he were one of the pimps, crooks, or the other scum that Travis hates.

Travis's *Need* on one hand ("to be seen") and his *Public Persona* on the other hand ("to be invisible") collide. As the choices Travis makes force his *Need* and *Public Persona* into greater opposition with each other, *Taxi Driver* climaxes in an explosion of violence. In those violent moments, Travis sees himself as invincible: an idealized savior protecting Betsy and rescuing Iris. That violence, with its psychotic grandiosity, is Travis's *Tragic Flaw*.

THE BOILING POINT

Like all stories, *Catch Me If You Can*, *Monster*, and *Taxi Driver* move their protagonists from conflict to crisis and then to climax. The force that propels Frank, Aileen, and Travis through these circumstances—the force that propels all characters through every story—is their *Need*. As a story's circumstances tighten, a character's choices narrow, and the character's *Need* continues to go unfulfilled, the *Need* has nowhere to release itself. The *Need* is still pushing; but now, even the character's *Public Persona* is in the way. The *Need* is pressed under the collapsing *Public Persona* by the crushing weight of *Tragic Flaw*. In those climactic moments, the *Tragic Flaw* carries the greatest danger for the character. The *Tragic Flaw* also holds the greatest potential for redemption if the pressure of that jam-up can be relieved.

In *Catch Me if You Can*, Frank makes a climactic choice. He can keep running and continue trying to be everyone; or he can stay still, look at himself, and admit who he really is—a crook like his dad, and a cheat like his mom. Frank chooses to work with the FBI and serve out the rest of his sentence. Though he may not like it, he's made a step towards fulfilling his *Need* "to have his own identity." He now knows that as a convicted felon turned FBI informant, he's now no more an airline pilot than he is a James Bond. Frank fights his *Tragic Flaw* and wins.

In the final moments of *Monster*, Aileen has resigned herself to her fate. "Love conquers all, every cloud has a silver lining, faith can move mountains, love will always find a way, everything happens for a reason, where there is life, there is hope—oh well, they gotta tell you somethin'." Heartbroken by **Selby's betrayal, Aileen waits, still an ostracized loner, for the** ultimate legal form of abuse: execution. Aileen dies a victim. Her *Tragic Flaw* has won.

TRUTH

Selby's betrayal, Aileen waits, still an ostracized loner, for the ultimate legal form of abuse: execution. Aileen dies a victim. Her *Tragic Flaw* has won.

A series of newspaper clippings and a grateful letter from Iris's father tell us that Travis has survived *Taxi Driver's* climax. He's on the path to his *Need* being fulfilled; he's a hero in the newspaper and in the hearts of Iris's family. Yet, when he runs into Betsy in the final scene of *Taxi Driver*, he rejects her. His loner mask is still partially in place. He still sees himself as a grandiose savior as much as a marginal loser. Travis remains trapped in his *Tragic Flaw*.

Travis Bickle's *Tragic Flaw* of violent grandiosity erupts several times during *Taxi Driver*. Aileen Wuornos abuses victims and is herself abused over the course of her journey to the gas chamber in *Monster*. Frank Abagnale's masquerade goes beyond boyish thrill seeking long before the climax of *Catch Me if You Can*.

The *Tragic Flaw* is always visible in the choices a character makes. It's there whether it's only visible in a story's climax or is obvious from the start. A story's circumstances push its characters from conflict to crises; and those crises reveal who those persons really are. Do they sink into their *Tragic Flaw*, or do they overcome it?

The same is true for most human beings.

For the classical Greek dramatists who coined the phrase, *Tragic Flaw* (or *hamartia*) was an innate part of a character's identity. Whether noble like Antigone's martyrdom, heroic like Achilles's pride, or selfish and destructive like Agamemnon's ambition, a Greek protagonist's *Tragic Flaw* is always there in the character from the beginning, focused through a story's conflict, and what ultimately is behind the character's redemption or destruction in the story's climax.

Oedipus — Oedipus Rex
Need: "To be a child"
Public Persona: "To be a king"
Tragic Flaw: "To continue a cycle of incestuous abuse"

The basic concept of *Tragic Flaw* has remained the same for the entire history of drama. Mythic hero or everyman, any character that carries a *Need*, and has a *Public Persona* to cover that *Need*, has a *Tragic Flaw* scaled to that *Need* and to the *Public Persona* that covers it.

Howard — *The Aviator*
Need: "To be mothered"
Public Persona: "To have no limits"
Tragic Flaw: "To go crazy"

Leticia — *Monster's Ball*
Need: "To be loved"
Public Persona: "To porcupine everyone; to push everyone away"
Tragic Flaw: "To be a victim"

Bob — *Lost in Translation*
Need: "To be pure and honorable"
Public Persona: "To be a hustler"
Tragic Flaw: "To hate himself"

Vivian — *Pretty Woman*
Need: "To be special"
Public Persona: "To sell herself to others"
Tragic Flaw: "To devalue herself"

Alonzo — *Training Day*
Need: "To be somebody"
Public Persona: "To be a pig"
Tragic Flaw: "To terrorize"

Whether performing a character in classical drama, contemporary theater, film, or television, an actor must acknowledge that every human being, like every character, has a *Need*. But from the beginning of time, man has had a contempt for the expression of *Need*. So, as we grow, we cover *Need* with a *Public Persona* that offers the world the face of someone without *Need*. In spite of the cover, a *Need* continues to seek fulfillment. The *Need* inevitably becomes jammed up, because the *Need*, though hidden, remains too relentless to be contained by the *Public Persona*.

The relationship between *Need* and *Public Persona* is on the whole a constructive one. It's what defines our personalities. Although it's an unconscious process, the formation of a *Public Persona* to cover our *Need* is still a creative Process. *Tragic Flaw* is the latent destructive potential that exists in the relationship between our *Need* and our *Public Persona*. If we remain oblivious to the jam-up of *Tragic Flaw*, we are effectively self-blinded and doomed to walk the streets like Oedipus.

SUSAN BATSON

THE TOOLS

Using *Need*, *Public Persona*, and *Tragic Flaw*, an actor can make any character reach any audience, regardless of language, era, theme, or style. The actor who masters these three dimensions of character becomes equipped to create life out of a script. But in order to make a character live and breathe in all three dimensions, you—the actor—will have to confront the same three dimensions in yourself.

It's easier for most people to lie about their *Need* than consciously to admit that it even exists. We can escape the destructive jam-up of *Tragic Flaw* by admitting to the truth of our *Need*. But it's not easy. Allowing the *Need* to live out in the open, and taking responsibility for it may become a daily struggle; but all who wish to live freely and honestly should take up the challenge to discover and examine the *Needs*, *Public Personas*, and *Tragic Flaws* within themselves.

By unpacking a *Need*, *Public Persona*, and *Tragic Flaw* of your own, you will be able to take everything you are as a human being, and give it over to a character. If you have enough courage to overcome the fear that comes with inward exploration, you will gain indispensable creative tools for building a character. Through this process of discovery, you may even find new ways of building your own character and of identifying and maintaining your own moral center.

PART

II

THE ACTOR

CHAPTER SIX
THE INSTRUMENT

The actor is at one and the same time both the artist
and the tool of the art. His means of expression is himself.
Vera Mowry Roberts, *The Nature of Theatre*

CONDUCTING ELECTRICITY

Since 1947, Eva Marie Saint has contributed memorable
work to films by Elia Kazan, Alfred Hitchcock, Otto Preminger,
John Frankenheimer, Vincente Minnelli, Wim Wenders, and
Bryan Singer. When asked if it was difficult adapting to the varied
demands of these strong-willed directors, Saint said, "At the
Actors Studio, Lee Strasberg taught us that we the actors are
instruments, and the director is our conductor."

In my own work, I've auditioned and evaluated actors from
every background, of every physical type, and with every
conceivable level of training. I think of the total package an actor
presents as the actor's *instrument*. Looking at that instrument
helps me to understand and appreciate that actor's potential no
matter how raw the actor may be. And whenever actors can take

steps back, look at themselves, and assess their own instruments' strengths and shortcomings, they will become better prepared to take responsibility for their craft.

Every actor's instrument has these six qualities in varying strengths and proportions:

1. **Physicality**
2. **Intelligence**
3. **Imagination**
4. **Emotion**
5. **Sensory Faculties**
6. **Empathy**

Every actor I see, whether it's in class, in private consultation, or up on screen, has an instrument that employs some combination of these six qualities. Most actors embrace some qualities more than others. The very few true geniuses of the craft have instruments that blast out with all six.

PHYSICALITY

Every actor possesses a unique, physical nature. An actor with real star power freely incorporates personal physicality into a character. That doesn't mean that you have to be an Adonis. Porn stars sell tickets with their bodies; but that doesn't make them actors. Personality actors, stars like John Wayne (a former college football star) or Arnold Schwarzenegger (a former competitive bodybuilder), have a recognizable walk and a charismatic way of moving that they bring to every role—but not much else. The personality actor uses the body to decorate rather than to communicate a story.

Truly potent star-power physicality transcends age. Warren Beatty and Jack Nicholson were both born the same year. They're both terrific actors and full-blown movie stars with four-plus decades of experience. Beatty is gorgeous; but his instrument doesn't physically communicate with the same timeless, feral quality that Jack Nicholson's instrument does. As years went by, Beatty has moved behind the scenes and doesn't work much as an actor, anymore. But Nicholson has hardly slowed down at all. His waistline may have grown, and his hair may have thinned; but Nicholson's instrument has remained physically open and vital. That animal physicality allows him to continue creating characters with the same volcanic intensity that made him famous in the '70s.

Christopher Walken's instrument has a timeless physicality as well. Walken has retained the disciplined, graceful motion he learned as a dancer. That hard-earned effortlessness is a distinctive physical foundation for his characters. His instrument's physicality colors all of his performances.

Acting is about transformation—using the craft of acting to create a character out of an actor. The personality actor's transformation is through a change in wardrobe. Great actors transform themselves by any means they can find. Lon Chaney was a hugely popular star in 1920s Hollywood. Chaney, "The Man of a Thousand Faces," went to grueling lengths to physically change himself into characters like Quasimodo in *The Hunchback of Notre Dame*. His commitment to using his body to transform into the roles he played was so strong that the straps, hooks, and belts he used to bend himself into a part permanently damaged his spine.

Chaney had an insatiable desire to create using every last bit of his physicality. He was the son of deaf-mute parents, and spent his childhood communicating with his family solely through gestures and physical movements. Chaney's emphasis on his instrument's physicality and his body's ability to transform and communicate began out of necessity.

Robert De Niro packed sixty pounds onto his slender frame to play Jake La Motta in decline during the second half of *Raging Bull*. The transformation allowed De Niro to break down any barriers that existed between himself and his character. De Niro's transformation helped collapse nearly thirty episodic years of La Motta's life into just over two hours.

Since De Niro is justifiably one of the most famous actors of his generation, his much publicized weight gain has become the benchmark of commitment and transformation for every working actor. But physicality is only one part of the actor's instrument. In their rush to duplicate De Niro's transformation, I think some actors obsess over their character's exterior at the expense of the character's interior.

INTELLIGENCE

Sarah Bernhardt remains one of the most famous actors of nineteenth-century theater. Women of Sarah Bernhardt's day were expected to be decorative. The "true" nineteenth-century woman possessed poise, perfect posture, and measured, graceful movement. That's what Bernhardt gave her audience.

Bernhardt's stately, mechanical femininity masked a woman who strongly identified with the ambition, control, and drive for success of the male-dominated Victorian age. "I do not prefer male roles," she said when asked about her portrayal of Hamlet, "but I do prefer men's brains." Before her acting career took off, Bernhardt supported herself with her body as a courtesan. And once she became hugely popular, she was a one-woman industry. She maintained her own theater, and controlled a repertoire of popular plays that she personally commissioned.

Bernhardt conducted her career with ruthless intelligence. Her genius was for self-promotion. But the modern actor's responsibility is to apply a ruthless intelligence to a character. You have to use your head to make smart, specific, and truthful choices that embrace your character, the circumstances, and the story. Your instrument must have the flexibility to hop from possibility to possibility to arrive at a strong choice.

In *Ocean's Eleven*, Brad Pitt's character, Rusty Ryan, almost never stops eating. In scene after scene, and after every plot twist, Ryan wolfs down buffet plates and shrimp cocktails. While I don't know what Pitt's precise intention was (it's not in the script), disclosing Ryan's compulsive appetite was a smart choice. His eating was very human, real, *Need*-based behavior that played against Ryan's super-cool façade. It added depth to the character and a layer of psychological reality to the story.

Early in *The French Connection*, Popeye Doyle's Partner literally breaks in on Doyle in bed with a woman he picked up in a bar. Though tangled in the covers, Doyle has the same ratty coat he wears throughout the movie draped over him. Here is a character, this choice says, for whom work is everything. He never takes a moment off, even when in bed with a woman. As brought to life by Gene Hackman, Popeye Doyle brings the street with him wherever he goes. It's another great choice from a smart actor.

For the film *The Contender*, Jeff Bridges knew that he had to build his character with unusual warmth. President Evans had to have a trustworthy familiar maturity to match the story's modern fable quality. Instead of emulating JFK, Harry Truman, or Abraham Lincoln, Bridges chose to stay closer to home. Bridges based the character of President Evans, his mannerisms and his speech, on the person whom he respected most in his life—his father, Lloyd Bridges. The choice was brilliant. It single-handedly sold the film's fantasy of the White House as the only place in America where honest men still prevail.

IMAGINATION

In her essay "The Quality Most Needed," legendary Broadway actress Laurette Taylor writes, "Beauty, personality, and magnetism are not important in the equipment of a star when compared to the creative faculty of imagination." An actor's instrument is grounded in the physical and controlled by intellect; but it creates using imagination. Your imagination is a pair of wings. A powerful, active, constantly working imagination lifts the truth of your own experience and the facts of character circumstances into art.

In his memoir *The Good, the Bad, and Me*, Eli Wallach describes his first film acting experience, in Elia Kazan's movie *Baby Doll*. A key scene called for Wallach's character to explode with rage when he sees the smoldering ruins of a Mississippi cotton gin. The camera was tight on him. The emotion would have to come from a real place. At first, Wallach balked. Where was the emotional reality of the scene? As a Jewish kid from an Italian neighborhood in Brooklyn, "all the cotton gins in Mississippi could burn down," he remembers thinking, "and I wouldn't give a damn."

As the scene was being lit, Wallach looked for a way to experience the necessary emotions. "I turned my back to the camera and thought, 'What if? What if a friend burned down my house with my wife and children inside?' Then I slowly turned, my eyes were tearing up, and I was filled with hate."

Asking "What if?" is the simplest way to access the imagination. Asking "What if?" Stella Adler says, "will turn on your ignition."

Acting requires faith. "You just have to believe," Humphrey Bogart maintained, "that you are the person you're playing; and that what is happening, is happening to you." An actor's imagination, rooted in an unshakable belief system, can triumph over almost anything. "Once that belief becomes a deep conviction," Muhammad Ali once said, "things begin to happen."

I worked with Milwaukee Bucks (later Seattle Supersonics) guard Ray Allen on Spike Lee's *He Got Game*. Denzel Washington is many things, but he's not a five-time NBA all-star like Ray Allen. He played basketball at St. John's, but that was in the '70s. He's kept himself in shape, but he's still more than twenty years older than Ray.

While shooting the climactic father-son one-on-one game between Denzel Washington's character Jake Shuttlesworth and Ray's character Jesus Shuttlesworth, I witnessed a miracle of belief. When the cameras rolled, Denzel landed his first shot right through the hoop. He did the same thing with his second, third, and fourth shots. The scene called for Jesus to beat Jake, but Denzel had psyched himself up so much and believed so strongly in his character's ability that he dominated Ray. Spike Lee had to call "Cut!"

"I didn't think I had to coach you on how to play the damn game" I said to Ray.

"Denzel got game, Susan," Ray replied.

"No, Ray," I told him, "he's just a fucking great actor!" Denzel believed. As long as Denzel Washington was acting—running on pure belief—he was unstoppable. As Jake Shuttlesworth, Denzel combined a bottomless will with some skills and came out on top. My guess is that if he'd faced Ray one-on-one as Denzel Washington, he would've been smacked down in a heartbeat.

EMOTION

John Wayne built his image well. Unlike Clark Gable, Jimmy Stewart, and many other of his leading man peers, Wayne avoided the draft in World War II. Instead, he remained in Hollywood, where he perfected a super-patriot *Public Persona* in war movies rather than in actual combat. When a role lined up with his personality, as in John Ford's *The Searchers* and *The*

Quiet Man, and Howard Hawks's *Red River*, Wayne displayed flashes of vulnerability. Cast as Rooster Cogburn in *True Grit*, Wayne wore an eye patch for the entire film. It was a personality actor's way of sustaining vulnerability for two hours. The Oscar Wayne won was as much for the eye patch as for his personality.

An actor's instrument has to create vulnerability and emotional sensation from the inside. Playing Cathy Whitaker in *Far From Heaven*, Julianne Moore dug underneath Cathy's frozen suburban trophy wife *Public Persona* and got at the vulnerability of Cathy's *Need* "to be loved." The tear that Moore cries after she says, "No one would know us there," while pleading with Raymond Deagan, reveals that vulnerability. Moore's instrument's ability to translate that emotional sensation told the story. It said more than any amount of begging, beseeching, and explaining could ever do.

Civilians believe that an actor reads a script, picks a feeling, and... emotes. But acting is not emoting. Acting is DOING. The actor doesn't express emotions, or grab at emotional results that correspond to what's described in the text. What the actor does is to release the truth of a sensation.

Thus, actors don't wonder how to force themselves to cry. Instead, when preparing, they ask themselves, "What is the sensation of loss? How and when have I had that sensation before?" For an actor's instrument, emotion is the capacity to actively create and release sensations. You recall that sensation actively and then release it. Perhaps it's tears. Perhaps it's laughter or a howl of pain. It could be anything, as long as it is an intimate sensation.

Actors have to know they have permission to expose themselves through their character. A lot of smart actors with good physicality and great imaginations still bottle up and won't let themselves actively experience and release an emotional sensation. They just don't feel safe enough to do it. Russell Crowe has no difficulty giving himself permission to release emotional sensation. In fact, he knows, like all great actors, that letting that sensation out is what his audience expects.

"I want to bring actual tears to their eyes," he has said in interviews, "and goose bumps to their skin."

Late in *The Insider*, Crowe's Jeffrey Wigand sits alone in a hotel room. His marriage over, his family in ruins, Wigand is "used up, broke, and alone." Crowe's instrument releases his character's pain with absolute clarity. Wigand doesn't say a word, but the sensation of brutal personal loss pours out of Russell Crowe's instrument.

SENSORY FACULTIES

Ray Charles's album *Modern Sounds in Country and Western Music* changed popular music. A black man making an LP of country covers was unheard of in 1962. But Ray Charles brought something new to songs by country stars like the Everly Brothers and Hank Williams. Ray Charles brought *himself*.

"When I do a song," Ray once said about doing cover songs, "I must be able to make it stink in my own way." Ray was able to put a layer of his own sweat and grit on squeaky-clean Nashville tunes.

In our daily lives, we naturally filter out most of the smells, tastes, colors, and sounds that threaten to overwhelm us. Actors do not have that luxury. The physical world around us is what gives our work the same stink of reality that Ray Charles's music has. Connecting with a character's sensory world gives an actor a tremendous advantage in the pursuit of truthful acting.

As DJay in *Hustle & Flow*, Terrence Howard surrenders to physical sensation with absolute ease. His South Memphis hustle channels the heat and humidity of a Tennessee July into his character. DJay has the realism and funk of the streets because Howard's instrument stayed open to the truth of the rock-bottom sensory world around him. The great actor's instrument not only can feel those details, it can store physical sensation, recall it, and release it, depending on the demands of the script.

EMPATHY

Physicality, intelligence, imagination, emotion, and sensory faculties, are all indispensable parts of the actor's instrument. But empathy—a generous psyche that naturally steers clear of judgment—is vital to the actor's art. It's a privilege to share your skin with a character. No matter how much the other characters in a story and the narrative point of view of the script itself may minimize the role you play, you simply cannot afford to judge or belittle your character yourself. Even if you're playing someone who in real life you would shun or attack, you still have to suspend judgment and let your instrument go to work breathing life into the role. Holly Hunter says, "I always feel that I am the advocate for my character. I'm there to protect my character."

Actors must recognize their responsibilities to the human beings they're given to play. Your instrument's empathy must therefore be intimate, precise, and available at all times. Nothing should stop you from preserving a compassionate connection to your character.

An instrument with really strong empathy goes beyond conscious judgment. Silent movie comedians like Charlie Chaplin and Buster Keaton understood this. They radiated empathy. Their instruments were so empathic that they could communicate story more fluently and truthfully than many contemporary actors can in full voice.

Most modern comic actors come from stand-up and sketch comedy backgrounds. They may understand who they're playing well enough not to judge their character; they may have the skill to physically embody a character; they may even be able to release emotion and conjure up the sensory world around their character; but if they don't *feel* the character, there's not enough there for an audience to grab onto.

On the set of *I Think I Love My Wife*, Chris Rock would often say, "This one, I know," about his character Richard Cooper. Chris and his co-writer Louis C.K. tailored the character of Richard Cooper specifically for Chris; and as he shot the film, Chris accepted and connected to the Richard Cooper inside him.

Richard Pryor epitomized the gift of empathy. As a stand-up comic, Pryor's intelligence was unbeatable. And as an actor, his physicality, intelligence, imagination, emotion, and sensory connections were all off the charts. No matter who he played, Richard Pryor always preserved a tender spark of humanity for his character. Pryor was originally hired to work for a single day on *Lady Sings the Blues*. But his instrument was so in tune that the film's producers expanded Pryor's screen time. His character spans the entire film. He was never given a proper name; but Pryor's "Piano Man" dominates every scene he's in. It's not because he was louder or funnier or had any more lines than anyone else. It's because—of everyone in *Lady Sings The Blues*'s cast—Richard Pryor's instrument carried the most empathy.

CHAPTER SEVEN
CHILD'S PLAY

The wolf shall dwell with the lamb, and the leopard shall lie
down with the kid; and the calf and the young lion and the fatling
together; and a little child shall lead them.

Isaiah 11:6

TRUE OR FALSE

No matter what an individual's process, training, or background may be, it is the actor's responsibility to tell the truth. Every great acting talent has recognized that simple fact. James Cagney, for instance, insisted that there was only one rule every actor must obey regardless of the character being played. "Always mean everything you say," Cagney once said. "Find your mark, look the other fellow in the eye, and tell the truth."

"The secret of art" writes revolutionary Russian actor, teacher, and director Konstantin Stanislavski, "is that it converts a fiction into a beautiful artistic truth." Stanislavski understood that actors bring characters to life by using the truth of their own experience. The actor's truth is the truth of honest *sensation*.

honest *sensation*. Some actors can find truthful sensation intuitively. But for those who didn't naturally work at that high level of sensitivity and creative freedom, Stanislavski had ideas about how to get there.

I've studied with some of the greatest acting teachers in the history of the theater. Several of these teachers—Lee Strasberg, Uta Hagen, Harold Clurman, and Herbert Berghof—were profoundly influenced by Stanislavski's beliefs and discoveries.

Despite their shared allegiance to Stanislavski, however, these great teachers' ideas and systems were all quite different from each other. They didn't teach acting the same way. They didn't even use the same words and terms to explain and describe the art to which they had dedicated their lives. One of the few things they had in common was that they understood the necessity for the actor to create and not to imitate. The actor must tell the truth.

These pioneers' names have become synonymous with the phrase, "method acting," a catchall term for any of Konstantin Stanislavski's ideological offspring. But gathering Strasberg, Hagen, Berghof, and Clurman (not to mention Stella Adler and Sanford Meisner—two other brilliant leading lights of modern acting with whom I did not study) under a single "method" banner is grossly inaccurate. Anyone who studied with them will tell you so.

THE INNER CHILD

My first audition was for the Boston Children's Theater. I was eight years old, and I had no idea that I was auditioning. My mother said, "These are the only people I know who can deal with you." I thought she had brought me to a mental hospital. Adele Thane, who ran the BCT, simply told me that my finger was bleeding. I randomly chose a finger—it was dripping blood—and I reacted. Even though my finger wasn't really bleeding, my heart was breaking at the thought of being abandoned by my mother. I was so convincing, that Adele asked me to join her group.

The way kids identify with the characters they make up, and the way that they completely give in to the sensations and laws of the worlds they create, requires the kind of openness and passion that adult actors train to achieve. Enthralled in their own imaginary worlds, children effortlessly transform themselves into characters. And they do it by playing.

OUT OF THE PAST

Another thing that all of the great teachers and directors I have worked with did agree on is that an actor must investigate and imagine every aspect of a character's psyche. I expect the same thing from every actor who works with me. The actor has to know every moment of a character's backstory and each detail of a character's physical life.

The way Herbert Berghof phrased it was, "You even have to know how your character shits and pees." No matter how irrelevant or mundane it might seem, he expected us to ferret out every detail of our role, whether the script dealt with it or not. Herbert's commandment got me thinking. If your actor must understand how your character would go to the bathroom, pick your teeth, scratch, snore, and anything else, wouldn't the best place to begin looking for honest physical and emotional details be at your character's most unselfconscious age?

"The child is the father of the man," wrote William Wordsworth. Who we are today is who we were as children. It's a simple truth that has been upheld by every culture for thousands of years. Buddhist iconography celebrates Siddhartha as the golden child. The image of Christ's birth and the Christ child are as resonant as the Crucifixion and Resurrection in Christian art and theology.

Carl Jung wrote of the "Divine Child"—an archetypal symbol of the power of innocence, hope, and promise. Emmet Fox, the theologian and philosopher, described the "Wonder Child"—the embodiment of limitless creative energy that exists inside every person.

The child inside is the part of our psyche that is ultimately alive, energetic, and creative. Though we hate to believe it, admit it, and use it, every act of creation and imagination begins with our inner child. In her book, *The Drama of the Gifted Child*, Alice Miller, a German psychologist, explains that the inner child is the custodian of our unfulfilled emotional *Need*.

Miller's book explains how the long-buried inequities of childhood aren't forgotten at all. "Everybody has a more or less concealed inner chamber that he hides even from himself," she writes, "in which the props of his childhood drama are to be found." Though hidden beneath our mask of *Public Persona*, unfulfilled *Need* follows us into adulthood and continues to define us. We soak in that unfulfilled childhood *Need* throughout our lives.

Despite the title, *The Drama of the Gifted Child* is not a book about the creative process. It never once mentions acting. Yet, Miller's observations confirmed to me that the key ingredient to effective creation of characters is *Need*. When I first read it, Miller's book was a revelation. It is required reading for all of the actors with whom I work.

An actor draws parallels between the truth of a character's *circumstances*—the *who* and *to whom*, the *what*, the *where*, the *why*, and the *when* that are spelled out in the script—and the truth of the actor's *own experience*. And the truest and most indispensable component of an actor's own experience is that actor's unfulfilled emotional *Need*.

For any actors to look beneath their own *Public Persona* and get at their *Need*, they must be able to peel back the adult exterior concealing their inner child. They must recognize that the child within expels the wellsprings of truth, imagination, and inspiration that comprise the foundation of all art.

The little boy or little girl inside each of us is also the part of us that is most vulnerable. By the time we are adults, we've spent our entire lives inventing and maintaining a *Public Persona* to cover the vulnerability our inner child represents. Letting go of that cover, surrendering the inner child to a character, and exposing it to an audience can be terrifying. But that surrender is the difference between good and great acting.

The actor who commits to communicating truth exposes the divine promise and the terrifying vulnerability of the inner child. That inner child is the center of an actor's creative strength because it is also the center of the actor's weakness. Truman Capote once said that actors are children. Actors can be children; but whether you're five years old or fifty, in order to act truthfully, you must connect with your inner child.

The ideas and exercises that follow are the first steps to committing to your greatness. Like any difficult endeavor, these steps require practice, practice, practice. But you will only see positive results if you can honor your inner child and create with a child's intensity of commitment while having fun with a kid's fearless spirit of play.

CHAPTER EIGHT

THE JOURNEY OF THE *NEED*

The longest journey of any person is the journey inward.
Dag Hammarskjold

A PAPER MOON

In 1972, director Peter Bogdanovich approached actor Ryan O'Neal about making a film called *Paper Moon*. It was the story of a 1930s con man named Moses Pray who is inadvertently reunited with Addie, a young daughter he never knew. Bogdanovich wanted Ryan's seven-year-old daughter Tatum to costar as Addie. Tatum had never acted before; but despite her father's anxieties and her own, they agreed to appear in the film together.

In order to keep things clear for young Tatum, Bogdanovich shot *Paper Moon* chronologically. The first scene, in which we're introduced to Addie at her single mother's sparsely attended funeral, was the first one to go before the cameras. The few mourners present include Moses, who has not yet revealed himself as Addie's father.

At the conclusion of the service, the presiding minister offers the supposedly orphaned little girl a cup of water from a pump. Lone wolf Moses reluctantly agrees to take Addie across the state to her aunt. When Addie hears this, she casually takes the cup of water from the minister and dumps it on the dry Kansas ground. It's a small but sharp gesture of defiance and a curt refusal of the minister's unsolicited help. Addie's rejection perfectly fore-shadows the partners-in-crime outlaw relationship she will shortly forge with her con man father.

And it was an ad-lib.

In front of a crew for the first time in her life, and barely able to read the script, seven-year-old Tatum O'Neal naturally created a moment that brought her character to life and moved the story forward.

"I felt very connected and perfectly calm," she recalls of that day in her memoir, *A Paper Life*. "I understood this little girl. I identified with Addie's bruised innocence, steely wariness, and above all, resilience. I knew firsthand what it would take for her to survive."

At seven, Tatum was so close in years to the formation of her *Need* that it was second nature for her to *drop in* to the bottom of the *Need*. Tatum unconsciously mined her own experience and naturally *dropped in* to her character.

RECONNOITERING

Anyone can recognize an emotional *Need* behind a *Public Persona* being presented to the world and the conflicted behavior that results when that *Need* and *Public Persona* jam in *Tragic Flaw*. An actor has to do more than just acknowledge these things. An actor has to explore *Need*, ferreting out as much detail and texture as can be recalled from the *Need's* birth and life and bring that truth to the character being played.

What came naturally to Tatum O'Neal at her age can remain elusive for an older actor. The years can secure the mask of a *Public Persona* so firmly upon us that we must really dig to make the connections and find the personal material that Tatum had at her fingertips.

To assist in that excavation, I have developed a process called the *Journey of the Need*. It's a way for an actor and me to work our way back to and through the actor's *Need*. Together, we identify useful triggers and parallels that the actor can use to create a character.

The *Journey of the Need* helps accustom the actor to uncovering and working with the rich gold dust of personal creative material that Tatum O'Neal was still living in at age seven. It grants actors the freedom and confidence they can only get by basing their work on their own truth.

A DREAM DEFERRED

Understanding the *Journey of the Need* calls for a demonstration. I'll therefore conduct an actor on the actor's *Journey*, pausing to describe what's being learned along the way.

So that the actor's discoveries will be clear, I'll put a fictional character in the hot seat, as if the character were an actor, conducting the Journey with **Walter Lee Younger**, the protagonist of Lorraine Hansberry's *A Raisin in the Sun*.

Walter Lee Younger is one of the great characters of American drama. Over the course of *Raisin's* three acts, he becomes nearly as real as anyone on any street or in any life.

Black, in his mid-thirties, living at home, and barely eking out a living for himself and his family as a chauffer in 1950s Chicago, Walter's life is a frustrating and humiliating daily struggle. He dreams of a better life for himself and his family. Walter's family—his wife, Ruth, their son, Travis, his sister Beneatha, and his mother Lena—are all packed together into the small tenement apartment Walter grew up in. The center of his dream of a better life is a sizable insurance check from his late father's life insurance policy. Lena has the money earmarked for Beneatha's education and a house where the Youngers can live and grow. But Walter's dream is to be an entrepreneur. He would use the money to invest in a liquor store.

It's not necessary to have read the play or to have seen it performed in order to follow Walter's course through the *Journey*. Just know that the biographical detail and personal material that Walter the "actor" and I will work with are real and true to him.

If Walter Lee were to walk into my studio, he would be equipped with everything necessary to do the discovery and exploration that an actor has to do. Together we could take the *Journey of the Need*, just as I have with hundreds of flesh-and-blood actors.

TRUTH

The facts and details Walter Lee Younger shares in his *Journey* are in the play. This information is true to the period in which the play takes place, and to the world Hansberry has created.

What follows is NOT a script. There are some words of dialogue from the play; but it's wholly my own creation, based on Lorraine Hansberry's story.

Consider it a transcript of a conversation: one that would take place if Walter Lee, the actor, came to my studio in order to learn how to act.

SUSAN: The work we'll do together here is based on *Need*. What do you think your *Need* is, Walter?

WALTER: Money! Lots of it. White people's money. Enough money that I don't have to say, "Yes sir, no sir..."

SUSAN: I understand where you're coming from. Lots of us need money. Let's call that a circumstantial need.

WALTER: What other kind of need is there?

SUSAN: A need out of your childhood's circumstances. Something that was formulated by the time you were five or so, and that lingers from that age. It's a need that still drives you.

WALTER: You're not listening! By the time I was five, my need was money—my need, my father's need, my mother's need...

SUSAN: Absolutely. But I'm more interested in a force inside you that propels you through your life.

WALTER: I'm not sure I'm getting this. You mean something I was feeling inside?

SUSAN: Yes. Something you needed...?

WALTER: I needed...like, respect. Like my father. Yeah, I needed to be somebody, like the Rockefellers. Not white, but I wanted—I mean I needed—that kind of respect. Like, when I was real little, I was thinkin' that my father needed respect, and he wasn't gonna get it the way he was going.

SUSAN: So you need respect: "To be respected"?

WALTER: Yeah, to be somebody...

STEP I — The Unfulfilled Place of the Need

Having established a childhood Need, the actor explores that Need by recalling and describing an experience at a time and a place that the actor associates with the Need.

SUSAN: Walter, do you remember a time when you felt like the lowest nobody in the whole wide world?

WALTER: Damn! I feel like that every day I put on that chauffeur's uniform.

SUSAN: Think if you have one event that stands out in your memory.

WALTER: Yup. I was six years old.

SUSAN: What time of year was it—summer, winter, fall?

WALTER: Winter. Always in the winter, I looked raggedy—sweaters with patches, y'know?

SUSAN: What time of day was it?

WALTER: Right after school.

SUSAN: Can you remember what you were wearing?

WALTER: Yup, 'cause I didn't have a lot of clothes. Brown pants—bad wool, they itched—brown sweater, like I said, patched up, good sewing but patched. A too-small, white button-down shirt that I washed every night and my mother ironed every morning. Really worn out, too...

SUSAN: What was the place? Were you indoors, outdoors?

WALTER: Inside the apartment. Same damn apartment we still live in.

SUSAN: Was it hot or cold?

WALTER: It was cold! It was always cold in the winter. Still is!

SUSAN: Do you remember any sounds? Any smells?

WALTER: How it smelled? Like... it smelled like greens. Greens cooking. Mama was making supper.

I'm interested in where the event happened, what that place looked like, and as many specific physical details as the actor recalls in describing the emotional experience of that Unfulfilled Place. Colors, sounds, music, the clothes the actor wore—any one of these things can become a trigger that will generate sensation in the actor. What we're doing in this step is a Sense Memory exercise. (We'll explore Sense Memory in more detail in the next chapter.)

SUSAN: Is there one thing about the apartment that day that you'll never forget? The lighting? The sound? A piece of furniture?

WALTER: The carpet. Bright colors—reds and browns. It looked rich, back then. There were no worn-out spots to cover. Not like now. I think one of the women Mama worked for gave it to her.

SUSAN: Good! What did you *Need* on that day?

WALTER: Respect! The teacher had asked us to think about what great American we wanted to be, and I said Rockefeller. The whole class fell out laughing. Even the teacher. Then she said, "Be realistic, Walter. You can be like Joe Louis, Jackie Robinson, but Rockefeller? Never!" I tried to explain I didn't want to *be* Rockefeller, but everyone just laughed and laughed, and I ran out of the room. I ran home and told Mama what happened. And she laughed, too.

Step II — Person to Whom You Unsuccessfully Go To Have the *Need* Fulfilled.

From the Unfulfilled Place of the Need, we move on to a person who was present, or with whom the actor associates the Need going unfulfilled. Again, we're looking for sensations amongst remembered details.

SUSAN: What's the strongest physical feature of your mother?

WALTER: How she looks at people. How she looks at me. Her eyes.

SUSAN: Strongest human quality?

WALTER: *Human* quality?

SUSAN: What she radiates when she walks into a room?

WALTER: Her faith in God. Sometimes I think she has no faith left over for me.

SUSAN: She laughed at you?

WALTER: Yes. And I died. I just crumbled inside, and died.

SUSAN: Was there something you wanted to say or do but didn't?

WALTER: I can be whatever I want to be! I can! I'm going to *be* a great man, someday. I got dreams!

[Walter covers his face, tears streaming down.]

WALTER: It stinks—this world stinks—a man's got dreams, and he can't... can't...

SUSAN: Can't what?

WALTER: Can't get near them—never mind tell nobody, 'cause they laugh at you...

SUSAN: What did you *Need* from your mother?

TRUTH

WALTER: Respect! I *Need*ed her to respect me, not laugh.

SUSAN: You went to her because you wanted respect. You thought she would fulfill your *Need*, right?

WALTER: Right!

SUSAN: Is there something she said in that regard? Something that you'll never forget?

WALTER: I'll tell you what she says: she says, "I don't want that on my ledger." Whenever I try to tell her about my dreams, share my dreams with her. "I don't want that on my ledger." Some list she's keeping with God. Something like that.

SUSAN: Is there anything you'd like to say to her but never have? Just have her stand right there in front of you. Speak to her...

WALTER: Mama, believe in me. Have faith in me! I'm the head of the family now! I'll take care of you better than Daddy. I'll take care of everyone when I get my business going.

Step III - Participation in the *Need* Going Unfulfilled

Step three asks the actors to examine their own behavior and identify the things they do (or fail to do) that may prevent them from having their Need fulfilled. Seeing the personal obstacles and conflicts in the actor's own life accustoms the actor to identifying the same traits in a character.

SUSAN: Why haven't you told her that?

WALTER: She'd just call me a fool, or laugh at me again. Isn't it enough that I don't get any respect in school, in the neighborhood? Do I have to ask for it in my own house? She should know—she *does* know, that's what a man needs. Even a boy. She's always saying how folks say the Youngers are "proud acting" behind her back. Why doesn't she let me act proud?

SUSAN: You've never told her that?

WALTER: She should know! She does know!

Though ambitious, smart, and capable, Walter Lee Younger says he's helpless to have his Need "to be respected" fulfilled. But he expects those whose respect he craves to simply recognize his Need and fulfill it on their own. He participates in his Need remaining unfulfilled by not communicating, by not speaking his mind in a way that the people who love him can understand. Like most people (and most characters), his unfulfilled Need is unconsciously self-maintained.

Step IV - The *Tragic Flaw*

Every life involves a constant tension between a person's Public Persona and the Need that it covers. And everyone has at least one Tragic Flaw, which erupts when the two jam up. In Step Four, I encourage actors to discover what their jam-ups are.

SUSAN: What happens when you can't go after your *Need* "to be respected"? What's it like when you can neither satisfy nor ignore it? When your *Need* gets blocked, I call it your *Tragic Flaw*.

WALTER: Tragic is right. But what do you mean, "flaw"?

SUSAN: A mistake, an error, a bad choice...

WALTER: I got it! Whiskey! I talk to the bottle. I hang out at the Green Hat, get a good buzz on, talk shit, and I'm okay... until next morning.

SUSAN: So you're an alcoholic?

WALTER: No, I ain't no alcoholic! I ain't got enough money... I'm not like those bums that are in the bar morning, noon, and night!

SUSAN: Then what's your flaw? Why get drunk and waste time at the Green Hat?

WALTER: Why not? Wouldn't you, if you'd been stepped on and laughed at your whole life?

SUSAN: You're a victim?

WALTER: Hell yes, I'm a victim. Like my daddy, my holier-than-thou mama, my wife...

SUSAN: Maybe that's a *Tragic Flaw*...

WALTER: What is?

SUSAN: Being a victim. Feeling helpless and trapped by a racist society.

WALTER: Hmm...

He's in his mid thirties and married; yet Walter Lee still lives at home—where he frustrates his wife, bickers with his mother, and mocks his sister's attempts to discover and better herself. Walter lazily sleepwalks through his job, whiles away his evenings at the local bar, and is of little use to anyone.

TRUTH

Walter's Public Persona is "to be a good boy"—subservient and invisible—a white racist's idea of a black man. That Public Persona can't hope to cover his powerful Need "to be respected." He is almost constantly in Tragic Flaw. Walter's Tragic Flaw is being a victim. He blames forces outside his control for the life he's actually made for himself. His missed opportunities and thwarted renditions are someone else's fault. Walter has surrendered to the racist society that crushes his spirit and for whom his powerless Public Persona is "to be a good boy."

Step V — The Child

A child whose Need went unfulfilled lies hidden just beneath the surface of even the most complex adult behavior. To establish a safe unity between the child within and the adult actor, I challenge the adult actor to imagine the actor's inner child.

SUSAN: Okay. Can you put your five-year-old child in front of you?

WALTER: Travis, my son? He's older than five...

SUSAN: No, I mean *you* at that age. The child that's still inside you. Can you see yourself as a five-year-old kid?

WALTER: Oh, got it. Yeah, I see him. I can see him. Me.

SUSAN: What's the greatest thing about him?

WALTER: Good-looking, real good-looking! ...No, wait. He got dreams. Yeah, a big dreamer...

By making a "promise to my child," I encourage the actor to realize that the inner child is an artistic strength, not a personal weakness.

SUSAN: What would be the commitment you would make to that little boy?

WALTER: What do you mean?

SUSAN: What promise would you make to him? Would you promise to keep him safe, make him happy?

WALTER: I'd promise that he'd get his dreams; that I'd help him make his dreams come real.

Walter Lee pledges to the kid within him to protect that child's dreams. The promise is a simple acknowledgment that helps the actor to remember that an inner child's vulnerability can be being safely accessed for the sake of creativity, and not displayed as some kind of therapy.

Step VI - Personalization of the *Need* Fulfilled

Just as there was a Person associated with the Need going unfulfilled, there is a Person who embodies the Need actually being fulfilled, even if it's just for a moment.

SUSAN: Walter, was there ever a time when you felt that your *Need* was fulfilled by someone?

WALTER: Fulfilled? You mean when I got respect from somebody?

SUSAN: Yes. Do you remember ever having that feeling? When someone made you feel respected? Even just for a moment?

WALTER: Well, that same day—that day when the kids at school laughed at me. Mama made it into a joke. But later, when Mama was asleep, Daddy came home. I told him the story. He was drunk, but he gave me a dollar and told me to save it so that I really would be Rockefeller when I grew up.

SUSAN: A dollar?

WALTER: Yeah, a silver dollar. Daddy understood for a minute. For a minute he saw me as the future, as somebody who was going to deserve respect.

Walter Lee connects through the feeling and memory of that person's strongest physical feature, human quality, and also through a word or phrase associated with the limits of that person's ability to fulfill the Need.

SUSAN: What was your father's strongest physical feature?

WALTER: His hands. They were strong when I was a little boy. Powerful. But that was before my baby brother died and the booze took over. After that they always shook.

SUSAN: Strongest human quality?

WALTER: Hmmm... Grief. Since I knew him, he was grieving.

SUSAN: Was there something he said or did that you will never forget?

WALTER: "The only thing that God gave the black man was his dreams, and children to make them come true."

SUSAN: Is there something you wished you'd said to him while he was alive?

WALTER: Yeah. I always wished I had the courage to grab him, and then hug him until he cried or laughed.

SUSAN: Is your *Need* to be respected still driving you?

TRUTH

WALTER: Like crazy! ...I think of stealing from my mother—even killing my sister. ...Crazy ...I want to hurt somebody... Sorry...

SUSAN: No, don't be sorry! That's all great stuff! It's those things that you can use as an actor! It would be perfect if you were playing Othello. Imagine Othello's *Need* "to be respected" as a black man married to a white woman and leading a white army.

Step VII - The Dream of The *Need* Fulfilled.

The final step challenges the actor to engage imagination in order to turn feelings into art by imagining a world in which the Need has been fulfilled.

SUSAN: Now, one more step: can you imagine what life would be like if your *Need* were fulfilled?

WALTER: If I had respect?

SUSAN: Yes.

SUSAN BATSON

WALTER: Mama would have her new house, my sister would be in medical school, Travis would for sure go to college, and Ruth would have a husband she could count on! I'd have a chain of stores with my name on 'em. I'd have a driver to take me around from store to store, instead of driving some white man around...

Walter's dream would be one in which he has the respect he craves; a world where the kid beneath his Public Persona shines through. Walter's Dream of the Need Fulfilled is a fantasy in which his get-rich-quick schemes pay off. He provides for his family, is a well-known success, and has the respect of his family and his community.

Walter Lee pictured his dream fulfilled quickly and clearly. But it's heartbreaking to see how many actors struggle and stumble with this final step. Most of us are accustomed to a life in which our Need remains unaddressed. We take the child within us for granted, and carry on as if our Public Persona is all that we are.

SUSAN: Do you still have the silver dollar your Daddy gave you?

WALTER: Oh, hell, no! No, I spent it on candy and funnybooks the next day! I was a kid, you know?

SUSAN: Of course.

TRUTH

What came to light in Walter Lee's *Journey of the Need* were the same things revealed in any actor's journey. The people from the actor's past, the emotions, the physical sensations, the objects, the words, and the sounds they recall—all become vital building blocks that the actor subsequently uses to create a character.

No two people are exactly alike; so no two journeys cover the same ground in the same way. Each step is a signpost, a guide for where to go next. There is no one destination on this journey; there is only the trip itself.

If I feel that more can be unearthed by going quickly through a step that has little resonance, and going on to another step, I'll skip ahead. If I feel that an actor is very connected to one of my seven steps, I'll stay there and figure out what that connection is. Working one-on-one with an actor, I follow my instinct and intuition and go with what's generating the most material. And it's the same with "actor" Walter Lee Younger.

We're not looking for a smoking gun that accounts for all the conflict in a person's life. Remember that the *Journey of the Need* isn't formally bound to my seven steps in a strict questionnaire fashion. I'm more interested in how deeply and truthfully the actor *drops in* to a *Need*, and then how the actor works with or against each step. I'm always conscious that what we uncover will feed the multiple characters that make up a working actor's life.

THE WORK

Acting is all about the work—the study, the preparation, the rehearsal, and the performance. In my process, the *Journey of the Need* is where the work begins. Part of an actor's responsibility to the craft is to maintain a kind of mental filing cabinet. The memories and sensations that pop for actors in their own lives are the experiences they can use for creating characters. The *Journey of the Need* is a way to create or to enrich that stash.

This information is of course highly personal. It's used to enable actors to do better work, not as a way to win arguments with directors or writers or other cast members. Even though what we unearth together on the *Journey of the Need* is completely indispensable, it must remain totally private.

As actors get comfortable with the process, they begin to appreciate the individual function of each step. What an actor acquires from step three, for instance, may be more relevant to that actor or to the particular role being played than step six. Down the road, the actor may learn to rely on one or two steps in order to connect with a personal *Need*, or with the *Need* of a specific character. The *Journey of the Need* provides signposts indicating how the *Need* travels in the individual.

The *Journey of the Need* isn't an easy road. Many actors choose to avoid it. They'll hide from the revelations that are the byproducts of reliving the events surrounding their own *Need*. But if you can commit to the craft of acting, and if you are willing to give yourself over in the service of creation of a character, you'll embark on a journey of creative discovery and enlightenment on the road to your greatness.

TRUTH

Do you remember Brigitte Berry from the circle? She's lean and gorgeous and moves like Janet Jackson, Bruce Lee, and Anna Pavlova combined? Though spectacular, this Public Persona she displayed in the circle clearly suggests unfulfilled Need. Her movements lacked soul. It would be interesting to ask her what she thinks her Need is.

"I don't Need anything," she says.

"Nothing?" I ask.

"No, I've learned not to Need anything," she replies coolly.

I dig a little deeper. "Really? Absolutely nothing?"

"Like what I want, I get. Those other things like—..."

"Like what?"

"Like love. Understanding. Life's hard enough. I just don't think about that stuff. I have to look after myself."

"Do you want to be a great actor?" I ask.

"Of course I do! That's why I'm here. But what does that have to do with what I Need?"

She's not getting it. "Okay, what does it take to be a great actor?" I ask with feigned innocence.

"A good package. I'm smart and I get what I want. Oh yeah, I'm determined."

She leans back in her chair and crosses her long legs for effect.

"You've got what it takes to be a star, that's for sure," I tell her. "It remains to be seen if you have what it takes to be an actor. An actor has to be inspired as well as determined."

"Need, inspired—that's all a little too artsy for me."

"What do you have against art?" I ask her. "Isn't that what we're here for?"

SUSAN BATSON

"I'm here to work," she says, "pure and simple. Look. I grew up with asthma. Every day of my life, I woke up hoping I could breathe. Breathing—not wheezing, not panicked, not fumbling for the inhaler or for a shot; not seeing my mother weeping over me. She didn't have anyone to help her; no man, no insurance. She was the one who had the Need. She Needed for me not to be sick, okay? Figure it out—I didn't dare to Need. I just wanted to breathe. It was practical, really. I lived day-to-day, moment-to-moment. I just wanted to breathe. That's all I Need now...," she says, tears welling up in her eyes.

I smile and offer her a Kleenex. "You weren't lying," I say. "You really are here to work. 'To breathe' is your Need."

"Yeah" she says, blowing her nose.

CHAPTER NINE

SENSE MEMORY

You learn from a conglomeration of the incredible past—whatever experience gotten in any way whatsoever.
Bob Dylan

If you would understand anything, observe its beginning and its development.
Aristotle

THE REVOLUTION

Acting, nineteenth-century style, had little to do with creating a character. The thespian of the day ceremoniously posed and recited lines. The audience merely admired a player's great skill at formally speaking dialogue and methodically moving around the stage with mechanical precision. But in the early twentieth century, technology began to chase acting out of the dark ages. First the gas lamp, then the electric light, and finally the motion picture's flickering light revealed the rigidity and exaggeration of nineteenth-century theater for what it was.

At the same time, playwrights like Henrik Ibsen, August Strindberg, and Anton Chekhov sought to recast dramatic writing in a modern, psychologically realistic way. These new writers felt compelled to keep creative pace with what one critic of the time called "our tense, weary, high-strung, groping, restless age."

Audiences were ready to experience stories about flesh-and-blood people who shared their dreams, fears, and feelings. Storytelling had to shine light on people's inner lives, not just on their appearances. That responsibility fell to the actor.

"No declamation! No theatricalities! No grand mannerisms!" Ibsen wrote to a frustrated young cast member struggling with one of the playwright's complex characters. "Express every mood in a manner that will seem credible and natural. Observe the life that is going on around you, and present a real and living human being."

In order for drama to move forward, acting had to move inward. A visionary thespian named Eleanora Duse led the way ahead and led the way inside. She was the world's first truly naturalistic actor. After Duse, the craft of acting would never be the same.

THE MYSTIC

Eleanora Duse was born into a touring Italian theater family in 1858. Though raised on the tradition-bound nineteenth-century stage, Duse turned her back on the heavy makeup, pantomime gestures, and metronomic vocal delivery she learned as a child. She swept aside the stiff, old-fashioned acting style that separated an actor from a character.

"Her technique is the quintessence of pure, lived truth," wrote Italian playwright Luigi Pirandello. From classical and Shakespearean heroines to modern parts written expressly for her, Duse "lived her role with such truth that there seemed no distance between the soul of the heroine she was playing and the deepest parts of her own soul," said an adoring colleague.

Duse believed that there was a common human core that every character shared with every audience member. She saw herself not as a flesh-and-blood prop, but as a conduit for the essential humanity in everyone. "Of all of the actors," gushed a Milanese newspaper, "Duse is the only one who knows how to give a character human nature as well as symbolic nature."

Audiences and critics were helpless in the face of Duse's unwavering commitment and skill. "The shades of her emotion are evident even when she turns her back on the public," wrote a European journalist. "Her art lives totally within, a thing of the spirit," agreed the *New York Times*, when Duse debuted on Broadway.

Eleanora Duse's genius made her a superstar. Charlie Chaplin declared her "the greatest artiste that I have ever seen." Henrik Ibsen named the heroine of his *A Doll's House* after her. In 1923, two years before her death at age sixty-six, she became the first woman ever to grace the cover of *Time* magazine.

Duse's genius also generated controversy. Her repertoire included classic parts made famous by the charismatic traditional French actress Sarah Bernhardt. As Duse's fame began to eclipse Bernhardt's, the two became rivals. Theatergoers had fistfights in the streets of London and Paris over which artist, and which style of acting, was best. All over Europe, critics and audiences argued whether it was even possible to call Duse's acts of creation "acting."

But in pre-Communist Moscow's thriving theater community, Eleanora Duse's depth and realism became the gold standard for Russia's new generation of writers and actors. Anton Chekhov insisted that he could understand every word of her performance even though he knew no Italian. Seeing Duse for the first time, a Russian drama student named Alisa Koonan summed up the feelings of her peers: "If I can't act like her, I must give up the theater." One of Koonan's colleagues was even more impressed. His name was Konstantin Stanislavski.

STANISLAVSKI

When he first laid eyes on Eleanora Duse, Stanislavski was in the midst of organizing a new theater company: the Moscow Art Theater. This new acting ensemble would incorporate everything Stanislavski had learned in the decades he'd spent acting, directing, and teaching in Russia. Eleanora Duse's naturalism challenged Stanislavski. He believed that the effortless realism Duse brought to the stage should be every actor's goal. If the new science of psychology was now naming and quantifying human behavior, shouldn't it be possible to distill and codify the gift for acting that Duse naturally possessed?

But just how was Duse able to live so miraculously in a dramatic stage reality from moment to moment? Duse herself gave up few secrets. She said that her responsibility was to "live her art, not comment on it." Like many visionaries, Duse believed her ultimate purpose was God's will. Duse, her friend and biographer Eva Le Gallienne wrote, was "a mystic" who "sought, and served, and worshipped Him in and through and by her work." Craft and spirituality were one and the same to her. Duse resisted any attempts to demystify her approach. Like any great magician, she refused to reveal her secrets.

Though Duse offered few direct clues to a process or a system behind her phenomenal ability, she did occasionally confide in friends and admiring young actors. "I construct the entire character in my mind," she revealed in one letter. Her process, Duse said, was to "use everything in my memory, and everything that vibrates in my soul" in order "to conjure from the center and journey to the most secret heart of things."

Around the same time, a French psychologist named Theodule Ribot inadvertently suggested that Duse's admission might work as a strategy. In his book *The Psychology of Emotions*, Ribot observed that human beings store emotions and physical sensations along with the event that created those feelings. Memory and consciousness, Ribot said, are a complex, ever-changing melody of emotions, sensations, and events from the past that play counterpoint to what we experience in the present. Ribot coined the term "affective memory" to describe how our brain constantly revisits and recreates old hurts, fears, joys, and passions as we experience similar events in the here and now.

When *The Psychology of Emotions* was translated into Russian in the 1890s, Stanislavski became convinced that actors could harness the mind's natural tendency to build bridges between emotions past and present. An actor, Stanislavski theorized, uses memory to consciously recall the facts of the script: the words of dialogue, when to move, and when to speak.

Why then couldn't an actor recall and use personal sensations as well?

"Time is a splendid filter for our remembered feelings," Stanislavski would write in his groundbreaking textbook, *An Actor Prepares*. "It not only purifies, it also transmutes even painfully realistic memories into poetry." Stanislavski made affective memory the conceptual cornerstone of his new Moscow Art Theater and his Stanislavski System of acting.

Whether rooted in the Stanislavski System or not, all acting "methods" are based on communicating a character's experience with as much truth as humanly possible—not via imitation. A precious lucky few, like Duse, can do this naturally. For everyone else, there exist techniques and exercises that help connect the actors' truths—each actor's own experience, memory, imagination, and sensation—with each character's "truth."

TWO GIANTS

Many of the principles handed down from Stanislavski and modified, adapted, and changed over three generations are identified by a jumble of names and definitions today. "Affective memory," "emotional memory," "analytic memory," are all different terms describing **Sense Memory**—a process in which the actor uses the actor's own experiences to trigger genuine, truthful sensations in the character.

Inspired by Stanislavski's concepts, Cheryl Crawford, Lee Strasberg, Harold Clurman, and Elia Kazan founded the Group Theatre in New York City in 1931. Lee Strasberg and Stella Adler, two famous American acting teachers, each developed their own approaches to actors and acting while working at the Group Theatre.

Strasberg, a gifted academic turned actor, was drawn to Stanislavski's scientific, empirical examination of psychology and theater craft. Though Strasberg never met or studied with Stanislavski personally, he became convinced that truthful acting was tied to an actor's own personal history. After the Group disbanded, Strasberg devoted his life to championing the inward exploration that Stanislavski's teachings had inspired in him.

In an effort to distinguish his ideas from those of his teachers and colleagues, Strasberg initially described his approach as "my method of acting." The word "method" stuck. In the decades since Strasberg struck out on his own—first in the Actor's Studio, and then the Strasberg Institute—any program, process, or person that encouraged actors to use their own experience in the service of character has been misleadingly labeled "Method Acting."

Stella Adler disagreed with Strasberg's intense focus on personal history. She felt that an actor's experience was the actor's own business. Making the actor's emotional life the center of the creative process was an intrusion into the artist's privacy that Adler felt posed a potential psychological risk for the actor.

Like Duse, Stella Adler was born into the theater. She'd been onstage her entire life. As a young actress, Adler didn't use any system or set of principals to guide her. Strasberg was a brilliant theoretician and organizer. Adler was first and foremost an actor.

What's more, Adler eventually worked directly with Stanislavski himself. During several weeks of one-on-one work with Stanislavski, Adler discovered that the Russian master actually had a flexible and playful approach to the craft. Stanislavski believed that the ultimate solution to any creative challenge was the one that worked.

Stanislavski, Adler wrote decades after her experience in Paris, "made clear that an actor must have an enormous imagination, uninhibited by self-consciousness." When Adler became a teacher, she insisted that the actor's imagination, not past experience, was the key to creating real characters from a script. Strasberg, meanwhile, prized the actor's own storehouse of truthful experience and real emotion above all else. For decades, the two giants of American "Method Acting" sparred over Sense Memory and the actor's use of imagination.

But from today's distance, their argument is moot. The truth of your actor's own life—the sights, sounds, feelings, sensations, thoughts, and dreams you carry inside of you—are what stock your memory *and* fuel your imagination. It's a waste of actors' personal resources not to utilize the energy and authenticity of their own lives. And it would not become art if actors didn't lift that experience using their imagination. Sense Memory is a complement to the imagination, not an alternative to it. Imagination has to have fact and experience on which to feed. Sense Memory can provide those key ingredients.

My approach incorporates Strasberg's Sense Memory process. At the Actor's Studio, Strasberg would begin with a series of relaxation exercises. He would then ask an individual actor many questions to help the actor explore the past. It was a lengthy process, but it yielded useful information for many actors.

The Actors Studio was (and remains) a "theater laboratory," not a school. Actors like me were "members" not students. We gathered in "sessions"—not in classes—where we received instructions and notes from "moderators," not teachers. It was a safe haven in which we could explore an art form, not just to get stage experience and build acting chops. A movie set is not an acting laboratory, since an eighty-five-person crew is not going to wait on an actor doing a classic Sense Memory exploration.

I have streamlined Sense Memory into eleven steps that any actor can use individually. These are practical, finite questions intended to create connections between the given circumstances of a script and the powerful tools of an actor's own experience. You've already seen Sense Memory at work in Step One of "actor" Walter Lee's *Journey of the Need*.

To begin, the actor thinks back through memory to recall an event that carries an emotional sensation like one in a script. The actor then must ask these questions regarding that memory:

A. **How long ago did the event take place?**

B. **What was the time of year?**

C. **What was the time of day?**

D. **What was I wearing?**

E. **What did I *Need* in that moment?**

F. **What was the place? Outdoors, indoors, temperature, smells, sounds?**

G. **What is the one thing about the place that I will never forget?**

H. Was there a significant person there with me?

    a.   What was that person's strongest physical feature?

    b.   Strongest human quality?

    c.   Something the person said or did that I will never forget?

    d.   Something I wanted to say to the person, but didn't?

I.   Was there a certain behavior I kept repeating?

J.   Was there anything I wanted to say or do at that time but didn't?

    Release it now.

K. Why didn't I say or do it then?

To be clear: The goal of Sense Memory is to trigger **Sensation**—the gut response that generates emotion—not just the idea or the expression of the emotion itself. If you reach outside yourself to find out how an emotion should look, you're not being truthful. First comes the sensation. If the sensation is strong and honest, an actor will naturally communicate that emotion. Sensation first—everything else after.

Sense Memory is not a precise questionnaire or survey. It's a self-guided preparation that an actor uses to generate ideas and choices. When an actor definitively knows how to share personal experience with a character, the emotional events of the actor's life acquire a new power and value. Sense Memory allows the events of the actor's life to define the actor's work.

CHAPTER TEN

PERSONALIZATION

I've just seen a face
I can't forget the time or place
Where we just met.
John Lennon and Paul McCartney, "I've Just Seen a Face"

KISMET

I believe that there is serendipity in the way that actors and characters find each other. It's uncanny how the most celebrated film performances contain clear parallels between a character's circumstances and an actor's own life.

When Charlize Theron played Aileen Wuornos in *Monster*, her commitment was incredible. She physically transformed herself for the role.

Theron never showed a second of judgment or inch of distance from her character. In every scene, she gave her all, and didn't hold back one ounce of herself. Theron knew that the role belonged to her, that there was something inside of her that made Aileen true and real for her. As a child, Charlize Theron **saw her** saw her mother kill her father in self-defense. I don't know Charlize Theron, but I saw the movie. Her personal truth was up there on the screen.

Denzel Washington's mother sent her fourteen-year-old son to military school. She expected him to amount to nothing and thought military school would at least slow Denzel's descent into delinquency. In *Glory*, Denzel played Trip, a black soldier proving his worth through combat. By the time Washington was cast in *Glory*, he had been proving himself for his entire life. He knew everything there was to know about war and military history from his school days. Washington brought so much of himself to the role of Trip that it became his professional breakthrough.

The film *Five Easy Pieces* climaxes in a heartbreaking scene in which Jack Nicholson's character Bobby Dupea attempts a kind of reconciliation with his father. In the years since Bobby has rejected and abandoned his family, Bobby's father has had a paralyzing stroke. As the scene begins, prodigal son Bobby wheels his virtually comatose father out onto a hill at sunset. His asks his father if he's comfortable, then searches for words that might have some meaning for either of them.

"I don't know if you'd be particularly interested in hearing anything about me, my life," Bobby begins. "Most of it doesn't add up to much that I could relay as a way of life that you'd approve of. I move around a lot. Not because I'm looking for anything, really, but 'cause I'm getting away from things that get bad if I stay. Auspicious beginnings, you know what I mean?" Bobby searches his father's unresponsive face and continues,

"I'm trying to imagine your half of this conversation. My feeling is, I don't know that if you could talk, we wouldn't be talking."

In the wake of his breakout appearance in *Easy Rider* the year before, Nicholson's role in *Five Easy Pieces*, and particularly this scene, catapulted him into stardom. Though the rest of the film was written by Carole Eastman, Nicholson actually wrote the *Five Easy Pieces* son-to-father monologue himself. When asked by *Time* magazine whether he was invoking his own adoptive father in the climactic scene in *Five Easy Pieces*, Nicholson simply said, "The answer is, of course, I was." Jack Nicholson's fatherless childhood and Bobby Dupea's estrangement from his family were the tragic parallel truths behind one of the watershed scenes in American film, and a career-defining moment for one of the greatest American actors.

SEPARATION ANXIETY

When Laurence Olivier received an offer from Hollywood producer Samuel Goldwyn to star as Heathcliff in a screen adaptation of Emily Bronte's *Wuthering Heights*, he leapt at the opportunity. The director, producer, screenwriters, and literary source were all first rate. *Wuthering Heights* would be a prestige film—the perfect vehicle for Olivier to make his starring American screen debut. This would be an overdue leap forward in Olivier's screen career.

By 1938, when *Wuthering Heights* went before the cameras, Olivier had become a household name in his native England. But he was still nearly unknown in the U.S. The truth was that he'd been scouted by Hollywood five years earlier to play opposite

Greta Garbo in *Queen Christina.* Unfortunately, Olivier was fired by the star and replaced by Garbo's lover John Gilbert during the first week of production.

When *Wuthering Heights* began shooting, Olivier invested Heathcliff with all the leaping frenzy and athleticism that had made his recent stage interpretation of Hamlet a sensation in the UK. But after viewing dailies, Goldwyn declared Olivier's performance "stagy," "rotten," and worst of all, "not real for a minute!"

Director William Wyler was just as dissatisfied. Free with criticism but short on suggestions, Wyler shot dozens of takes of the same scenes. His only note to Olivier between each take was "Just be better!" Proud and frustrated, Olivier lashed out at the director, declaring that "This anemic little medium can't take great acting!" He regretted it instantly, as Wyler and his seasoned Hollywood crew burst out laughing.

Olivier, and his costar, Merle Oberon, also quickly grew to detest one another. They were playing two of the most famous lovers in nineteenth-century literature, but they fought and bickered incessantly on the set. Oberon accused Olivier of spitting on her during their love scenes. Olivier dismissed Oberon to her face as an "amateur."

Just a few weeks into production, *Wuthering Heights* was heading for disaster. At age thirty, Olivier's career couldn't afford a second high-profile dismissal. If he expected to ever work in Hollywood again, he would have to make Heathcliff as "real" as Goldwyn demanded. But how on earth could he convince an audience that Heathcliff's love for Cathy was immortal and enduring if he hated his costar, and was the laughing stock of his collaborators?

The answer lay inside him.

For months prior to his signing with Goldwyn, English tabloids had buzzed about Olivier's scandalous affair with a gorgeous young starlet named Vivien Leigh. In spite of both being married to others, the two had fallen hopelessly in love. Leigh even abandoned her infant daughter so she and Olivier could be together.

Olivier left England to shoot *Wuthering Heights* on Vivien's twenty-fifth birthday. He wrote her daily love letters to remind her of his ardor and the passion that they shared. He wasn't just lovesick at their separation; he was secretly terrified that, in his absence, Leigh would succumb to public pressure and return to her husband and child. Separated for the first time from the "pure, driving, uncontainable, passionate love" he'd found, Olivier felt alone, empty, and, in his words, "blind with misery."

Olivier's agony of separation and anxiety about commitment were the same as Heathcliff's. Olivier the man craved Vivien's love in spite of their separation by geography and scandal. Heathcliff the character desperately desired Catherine, in spite of their class difference and her marriage. To pull out of his acting tailspin, Olivier let the two become one. The man who decades later would be so dismissive of "method acting," as he understood it, rebuilt Heathcliff from the inside out.

"Merle and I had been spitting at each other all day in real hate," he remembered of his breakthrough. "I was most deeply in love with Vivien, and I could think of little else. Wyler suddenly made us do a love scene, which went beautifully in one take."

Olivier had cracked the character. In all his subsequent scenes with Cathy and tantrums without her, Olivier infused Heathcliff with the deep yearning and ongoing frustration in his own life.

Midway through the film, Heathcliff, grown to a prosperous manhood, is reunited with his beloved. But his ecstasy lasts only for a moment. What happens on Olivier's face as he says "Cathy," and then catches sight of the man Cathy has secretly married, is profound. His *sensation* of Vivien—the longing and the unrelieved pain of separation that Olivier the man knew all too well—is vivid and unmistakably true.

Though it was a torturous lesson, Olivier treasured what he learned. *Wuthering Heights*, he said years later, "taught me how to be real." It also illustrates a core acting concept called Personalization. Using Personalization, an actor deliberately does what Laurence Olivier did intuitively.

SOMETHING PERSONAL

You don't have to be separated from the love of your life to feel lost on a set. On any film, at any budget, the realities of filmmaking can conspire to force even the most valuable actor to work in the most inhibiting conditions imaginable.

Imagine that a script calls for your character to have a climactic, emotionally wrenching exchange with another character. The director decides to stage the scene first in a two-shot of the actors in the two roles together in the same frame, and then in a pair of close-ups, one of each of you, covering the same lines of dialogue.

The two-shot goes well. You've done your homework. You connect with the script, with the character, with yourself, and with the other actor. Now, it's time for the close-ups. The other actor—an Oscar winner and a pro—goes first. The camera shoots over your shoulder. Your face can't be seen, but you give it everything you have. Your costar responds with three different solid, complex takes in a row.

Satisfied, the director turns the camera around on you. It is time for *your* close-up. But your costar is on the way back to the trailer. "Sorry, darling," the other actor says to you with a wink. "All I had in me were those three takes. Nothing personal."

A grip sets up a light stand and a camera assistant puts a cross of colored tape on it at your costar's eye level. This is your scene partner for your close-up. You have to be just as truthful to a metal stand as you were with one of the world's greatest living actors.

Even if you've barely rehearsed or have made virtually no connection to the actor with whom you've been working (let alone a C-stand or a target on a blue screen), using Personalization, you can still be absolutely truthful. There are people in your life who hold a strong emotional sensation for you. Personalization lets you use that sensation to triumph over distracting practical realities on set and make the character's emotions and circumstances ring true.

When a Personalization is strong, even a C-stand can gain feeling and presence. Like Sense Memory, Personalization allows the actor to create parallels between his life experience and the character's circumstances.

SUSAN BATSON

A. Begin the Personalization exercise by examining a person from your life whom you associate with an unfulfilled *Need*. Ask yourself to remember:

1. **The strongest physical feature of the person.**
2. **The strongest human quality of the person.**
3. **Was there something the person said or did that I will never forget?**
4. **Is there something I always wanted to say or do to the person that I never said or did?**

In 1, the strongest physical features should be clear and simple. *Eyes, mouth, hands, hair*—the name should come easily. 2 asks for what the person projects—*warmth, fear, anxiety, love*— what is the name of that feeling? 3 asks what did you *Need* from the person? It's that answer that generates real sensation. You're looking for the kind of feeling that you can wield and use, not just explore and speculate about. A *Need* carries that kind of energy. In 4, you think of a solid, active thing that you wished you had said to the subject of your Personalization. You don't have to actually say it. Just knowing that there was something you should've said will lend focus.

B. Ask yourself what sensations the person you have chosen creates in you. Imagine the person in the room in front of you and address the person directly by completing the phrase, "I see you as...," reciting as many sensations as you can. Using his father as a Personalization, Walter Lee might say, "I see you as helpless,

I see you as not loving me, I see you as scaring me, I see you as a drunk, I see you as my future," etc. Had Olivier done an actual Personalization exercise for Vivien Leigh, he might have said, "I see you as my only desire, I see you as someone I have to trust, I see you as someone I'm afraid of losing," and so on.

C. Ask yourself what you *Needed* from that person. Say it out loud by completing the phrase, "I *Need*..." For instance, Walter Lee might say, "I *Need* you to see me, I *Need* your respect, I *Need* to know that you love me, I *Need* for you to have faith in my dreams." Olivier might say, "I *Need* you to love me as much as I love you, I *Need* to hear that you will never leave me, I *Need* for you to not play games with me, I *Need* to know that we'll always be together."

D. Finally, ask yourself what it is that you want the person to understand and to know about you and about who you are. Say it out loud by completing the phrase, "I am..." with the name of a sensation you experience. "I am sad, I am afraid, I am your son, I am somebody who deserves respect, I am a father, too, I am not going the way you did," are some of the things that Walter Lee might say. "I am your lover, I am afraid you'll leave me, I am lonesome, I am angry, I am insecure, I am faithful," would perhaps be part of Olivier's experience, were he to have done an actual Personalization exercise.

You are looking for a sensation. Acting is doing—it is activity. Again, *sensation*—an active moment in which the actor has an internal, gut experience—is what engages an audience and propels a story. Imagining the face of someone else over the face of another actor won't create sensation. Playing at a feeling won't reach an audience.

For Personalization to work, it's vital not only to actively experience a sensation, but also to NAME IT. In both Sense Memory and Personalization, you are working at creating a belief system. All belief systems depend on words. When you name a sensation, you own it. A name can help to ground and concretize a sensation so that it can be accessed over and over, in take after take, and performance after performance. The Personalization has to be thorough so that you get as much sensation as possible. As you name the sensation, the sensation becomes a tool, not just a feeling or a memory. A name is an active choice. It's a handle that lets you use the sensation of an actual person—what the person means to you, and how that makes you feel—to engage the story.

CHAPTER ELEVEN

THE SENSORY CONDITION

My senses discovered the infinite in every thing.
William Blake

How good is man's life, the mere living! How fit to employ
All the heart and the soul and the senses forever in joy!
Robert Browning

GOING IN STYLE

When he was cast alongside George Burns and Art Carney in 1979's *Going in Style*, Lee Strasberg had only been acting in films for five years. Despite directing and teaching for half a century, Strasberg's film debut had taken place at age seventy-three, when Al Pacino persuaded his teacher to take the part of Hyman Roth in *Godfather Part II*.

Going in Style's script called for George Burns's character, Joe, to go through a box of old photographs that belonged to his recently deceased roommate. Joe is overcome with grief. At the same time, his age betrays him. As he weeps for his friend, Joe wets his pants like a baby.

When it came time to shoot the pivotal scene, Strasberg was amazed at the simplicity and effectiveness of Burns's process. Burns made no fuss while getting rigged for the "gag." He asked no questions. The cameras rolled, the director called "action" and cued the special effects technician, and then Burns made the scene work. "If you can fake the truth," Burns once glibly riffed, "you can act." But there was nothing fake about his commitment to the physical reality of that scene. He knew what he had to do. He assumed the responsibility for the physical reality described in the script, and he went for it.

Actors don't just communicate story through their characters' emotions. An actor is also responsible for a character's reactions and responses to the physical world of the script. Every script gives a specific indication of the physical reality depicted in each scene. Igloo, desert, jungle, or library— it's right there on the page. Part of the actor's craft is to honor and maintain that physical reality—the **Sensory Condition**—of the scene, regardless of where or how the scene is being shot.

The actor uses the actor's craft to translate the physical world of the script to the audience. You translate your character's physical experience—what the character's five senses contend with in the scene—through your own body. George Burns had been in vaudeville, TV, and radio on both coasts for more than half a century. Burns had done decades of exploration and self-examination through constant and varied work. He didn't have to consciously translate anything. His understanding and his expression of the physical Sensory condition called for in the script was second nature to him. It didn't matter how potentially embarrassing it was. In fact, the sensation of shame that Burns communicated made the moment work all that much better.

Commitment to the physical world of a script is a difficult thing for some actors to sustain. Many performers, for whatever reason, are too inhibited to let themselves believe in the environment that the script spells out. For these actors, scripted circumstances involving heat, cold, exhaustion, thirst, and so on become elusive abstract concepts instead of the simple, ordinary Sensory Conditions that they are in real life. These actors can't use their bodies to translate those physical circumstances with the same truth with which they experience physical sensation every day.

Strasberg would address this block through relaxation techniques and sensory exercises. He believed that when an actor resisted the sensory world of a script, the actor had to physically relax. But I believe that when an actor can't experience a script's Sensory Condition for the character, it has nothing to do with being relaxed. Actors won't give themselves permission to feel the sensorial elements of life if they're not in their body.

No amount of relaxation will put you in touch with yourself as a sensual, sexual being. No breathing exercise will instantly open you up to the world of sensation that you've been unconsciously working overtime to keep out. As Eleanora Duse said, it's a matter of "sensuality evolving into spirituality." The actor's own vivid and real experience helps to sustain an unshakable faith in the physical world of the character. Thus, actors who can comfortably inhabit their own body will remain open to every kind of possibility of the senses.

IN GENERAL

Culture by culture, and nationality by nationality, human experience—the nuts and bolts of sensation, thought, and belief—remains the same. It doesn't matter what era or what society, we all share an essential humanity and recognize that humanity in each other.

An actor who uncovers the actor's own real experience, and who then gives it over to a character participates in that unity. Thus, when actors make Sense Memory, Personalization, and Sensory Condition true for themselves and their characters, they will communicate that truth to anyone watching. It makes no difference what genre, style, or era—the truth transcends language.

The craft of acting involves emotional and sensorial detective work; but your art of acting will be in the choices you make with those raw materials you've gathered. The actor has to BE SPECIFIC. To quote my mother, "Generalities are the things that make bigotry grow." Actors who carefully and honestly map out parallels between their own life and the life of their character using Sense Memory, Personalization, and Sensory Condition, don't generalize. They don't "play a feeling"—angry, sad, guilty. They don't "fake" being drunk, exhausted, hot, or cold. Sense Memory, Personalization, and Sensory Condition force the actors to specifically apply truthful, specific sensations of their own to a character's circumstances and to the story itself.

SUSAN BATSON

Using Sense Memory Personalization, and Sensory Condition requires that you dig. These principals will force you to bring your own experience into sharper focus than a civilian would ever attempt. There are no half measures in this kind of work. Truthful acting requires that you bring YOU to the table. It's a challenge, and it's a gift. When you use what you would otherwise hide or ignore to create a character, you will naturally gain at least some insight into yourself.

The last words on these ideas and techniques are Stanislavski's: "Create your own method. Don't depend slavishly on mine. Make up something that will work for you! But keep breaking traditions, I beg you."

CHAPTER TWELVE

THE FOURTH WALL

"Please keep your eyes trained to the balcony-rail level so I can see them." I obliged, playing straight out front, and, of course, totally lost a sense of privacy and reality.
Uta Hagen, *Respect for Acting*

STAGE AND SCREEN

Some experts insist that there's a difference between stage acting and acting for the camera. Elia Kazan, one of the twentieth century's greatest theater and film directors, believed that screen and stage made different demands on the actor. "Many effective actors do get away with faking, posturing, and indicating emotions on stage," he wrote in his autobiography, *A Life*. "It's difficult if not impossible to get away with anything false before the camera."

In my opinion, there is no difference. It doesn't matter if it's a camera lens an inch from the actor's nose or an audience of thousands in a sold-out arena—truth is truth. No matter what medium, the actor's job is to truthfully communicate the story.

"INTO-ME-SEE"

The truth that actor and character share is the truth of intimacy. We achieve intimacy when we are unguarded and accessible. Intimacy calls for openness. In intimacy, there is no guile. There is no self-consciousness. There is no thought of consequence as we let sensation spontaneously, actively, and truthfully release.

An actor's unguarded intimacy allows the actor's sensation to work for the character. It's that intimacy that holds an audience's interest and earns its empathy.

"If you really do want to be an actor who can satisfy himself and his audience," Jack Lemmon once observed, "You need to be vulnerable. You must reach the emotional and intellectual level of ability where you can go out stark naked, emotionally, in front of an audience."

Think of it as "into-me-see." The craft of acting requires actors to open themselves up and expose the truth of genuine sensation through their character.

Intimacy only exists where there is a sense of safety. It thrives where there are both familiarity and trust. These things are in short supply onstage or on set. It's hard enough sharing open intimacy with a single complete stranger, let alone a theater full of unknown faces—or a camera's unblinking eye at the center of a set crammed with lights and crew.

Al Pacino and Christopher Walken defend their intimacy vigorously. They insist that their eyelines be clear of onlookers. The eyeline is the actor's focal point for connecting to the area around the eye of the camera. The actor must tolerate grips, sound, and camera crews; but gawking spectators are so distracting that they can break the intimate connection between camera and character.

The edge of the stage and the potentially judging eyes beyond the footlights have terrified actors for centuries. The lie-detecting eye of the camera lens is just as intimidating and inhibiting. Together, the audience and the camera have made wallflowers and people-pleasers out of legions of actors.

A STRONG DEFENSE

How does an actor reconcile the seemingly irreconcilable requirements of being intimate and truthful with the necessity of being heard and seen?

Stanislavski recognized that an actor had this dual responsibility. He identified what he called a "circle of attention" that defines the character's immediate environment. When the actor uses the "circle of attention," the actor stays centered between the character's world and the audience's world beyond.

Lee Strasberg had a similar idea. At the Actor's Studio, we were reminded that there was a "sensorial ring" surrounding the actor and the character. If an actor reached out to the audience, Strasberg would remind us to remain within the "sensorial ring"—the physical limit where the character's reality met the stage's reality.

Uta Hagen, the visionary teacher and cofounder of the HB Studio, took these concepts one step further. She taught her students to use the Fourth Wall. The Fourth Wall is the place where a scene's reality ends and an audience's reality begins. In theater, the Fourth Wall is at the edge of the stage. In film, it's where the eye of the camera lens and other equipment and crew shatter the story's reality.

Hagen encouraged us to use our imaginations to fill the gap at the foot of the stage or in the missing parts of a film set. She put us in charge of defining the divider between the end of the story's reality and the beginning of the audience's or viewer's reality. Hagen challenged us to imagine the actual missing wall, ceiling, or landscape; and if necessary, to substitute images of objects, people, or places from our own lives that we could recall in great detail.

I took Uta Hagen's Fourth Wall further. As I experimented with her Fourth Wall concept, I realized that the strength of Fourth Wall was in *sensation*, not in the memory or detail of the images the actor chose. There are people, places, and things so vivid in our memories that we can conjure up the feeling of them when we speak of them. "It's like he's here in the room again with me now." "It's as if I were standing there, I remember it so well," "I can almost feel it in my hand."

Clichéd though they be, these statements are rarely made lightly. We all have the ability to have some part of our attention in the here-and-now seduced by past memory.

The key to using Fourth Wall, I found, was the seductive power of memory. If I selected someone, something, or someplace that I felt strongly about, the sensation of that person, thing, or place seduced me into feeling its power for me on my Fourth Wall. If the person, object, or place I selected carried *Need*, it had a reality and a magnetism that drew my concentration out towards the Fourth Wall. I would not become transfixed by the object or the person. I didn't obsessively seek to picture a place. I just let myself experience a flow of sensation in my body—a sensation of wanting to be with whatever it was that I had placed on my Fourth Wall.

THE WALL

To illustrate this, I conduct an exercise for my actors that explores Fourth Wall sensation and seduction. For the exercise only, I would ask you to think of a person, object, and place that have very strong sensations associated with them. The person must be someone from your life that is bound to an unfulfilled *Need*. Based on his *Journey of the Need*, I'd say "actor" Walter Lee would use his father. The object should be something that carries the same sensation of *Need*. A gift from the person; something shared, like a toy, a letter, or an article of clothing—for example, the silver dollar Walter Lee's father gave him. The third and final element of the Fourth Wall is a place. Like the person and the object, the place must create sensation in you. For Walter Lee, I'd suggest he use the part of his family apartment living room where his father's chair stood.

In the Fourth Wall exercise, I designate a side of the room that will be the edge of the stage or where a camera and lights would be. I ask you, the actor, to face that side—the Fourth Wall. I then ask you to name and describe the three elements—the person, the object, and the place—one by one. Starting with the person, I ask you the same kinds of questions we used to explore Sense Memory and Personalization. What about this person carries *Need* for you? How do you feel about the person? What does the person wear? What colors, textures, sounds, and smells do you associate with that person? As you describe the physical sensations you know, and the emotions that you carry for the person, I ask you to focus those sensations and details in the center of the Fourth Wall in front of you.

I would then ask you to explore the sensation of the object you've chosen. What is the connection between the object and the person at the center of your Fourth Wall? How does the object feel? Hot? Cold? When did you see it last? As you answer these questions, the sensation of that object and the *Need* it carries come out in your answers. I would ask you to focus the sensations on the right side of the Fourth Wall, alongside the person.

We would then work with the place. Where is it? What are its details? It's colors? It's sounds? Is it light or dark? Warm or cold? Do you recall sounds and smells from the place? What is the place's connection to both the person at the center of the Fourth Wall and the object on the right side of the Fourth Wall? I would ask these questions until you have enough sensation of the place to imagine it on the left side of your Fourth Wall. Again, it's a matter of seduction. Can you recall the object, the *Need* associated with it, and enough sensation to be seduced by it? The place, like the person and the object, has to seduce you into experiencing genuine sensation.

In the old swashbuckling movie, *Scaramouche*, a fencing instructor explains to his pupil how to hold a fencing foil. "Think of the sword like a bird," he says. "Clutch it too tightly and you choke it. Too lightly and it flies away." The Fourth Wall sensation needs the same balanced treatment. In the Fourth Wall exercise, you are not trying to vividly picture images of person, object, and place as if they were floating between you and the audience. You are also not attempting to catalog every feeling, rumination, and detail about those three elements and their relation to an unfulfilled *Need*. The exercise is designed to help you get a sensorial *taste* of the physical and emotional response that those three elements have for you. With practice, that small taste of sensation should be enough to seduce you out of the instinct to hide your intimacy, while holding you back from reaching out and pandering to the audience. It's daunting at first for some actors. They mistakenly think that they have to use all their energy to precisely picture the three elements in front of them at all times. But in Fourth Wall, a little sensation goes a long way. As long as you've fully committed to a Fourth Wall element enough to have some sensation of it, it will remain alive and well and available as sensation in your body.

Sensation and seduction differ in strength and size, depending on the choices that the actor makes. Walter Lee may experience more seduction from the sensation of his father's living room than from the silver dollar his dad gave him. Or, in actual practice, it may be the other way around. The joy of acting is the joy of creation and play. An actor is always free to combine fact with imagination. The important thing is to use the Fourth Wall exercise to explore different qualities of sensation, seduction, and intimacy that originate with your experience and are put into use by your imagination.

MAKING THE CALL

To further explore the Fourth Wall, I ask the actor to improvise a phone call to the person used in the actor's Fourth Wall exercise. There are undoubtedly words the actor would like that person to hear, whether the individual is alive or dead.

The Phone Call demands that the actor fully communicate the sensation gotten from the person on the actor's wall. During the Phone Call, the actor experiences what it's like to speak with the immediacy of *Need*. It's a revealing test of an actor's ability and willingness to *drop in* to the intimacy. The Phone Call also requires that the actor use imagination to truthfully say what no one could possibly get away with in real life.

Usually, when people talk on the phone, they'll involuntarily drop their head and press the phone into their face. If the sensation from the actor's Fourth Wall is seductive enough, the actor will keep head up and face visible during the Phone Call, and will stay focused on the call itself, not on the audience. The Phone Call and Fourth Wall together remind the actor to always take responsibility for being seen and heard, while remaining intimate and open at all times.

Since Walter Lee used his father as his Fourth Wall persona, I'd ask him to also use his father as the subject of a Phone Call.

WALTER: Dad...is that you? Yeah? I'm fine, Dad... No, I'm not. I need you. Yes, I do, 'cause I ain't doing it right, Daddy. ...I'm hurtin' a lot of people. I don't mean to, but I am.

Walter instantly drops in to his Need and from Need to Tragic Flaw.

TRUTH

WALTER: You told me, "The only thing that God gave the black man was his dreams, and children to make them come true." Well, I got dreams, and I'm your child tryin' to make those dreams come true. But Mama—she won't let me have those dreams. She don't want my dreams on her ledger. Some kind of list she says she's keeping for judgment day.

Walter's intimacy is clear. The sensations of both his father and his mother change his voice, his expression, and his posture as he experiences them individually.

WALTER: Dad! It's so hard. Too hard. It makes you want to cheat, lie, steal, and kill. I'm a man with a family, a beautiful son. But we live in a rattrap! We're still sharing a bathroom with the rest of the people on our floor.

Still connected to his Need, Walter's words have strong sensation attached to them.

WALTER: You gave me that home. What kind of man were you? You had a family, too. But you drank too much, had too many women, and ruled us like you were some dictator. And then, Daddy, you gave up. You gave up when baby Claude died. You were nothing but a shadow of a man after that. Where did it get us? Mama's still cleaning white people's toilets, and I'm drivin' them around. She has a dream about getting a house, us all living cozy, but she doesn't understand a man's dream! I'm a mean, greedy son of a bitch because I have a dream. My family hates me!

SUSAN BATSON

His pain is real, but he's not running from it. The Fourth Wall sensation of his father keeps his emotional release specific.

WALTER: But I'm not gonna die like you, Dad! I'm not dying a bum with his head bowed low in shame, full of pain, can't even look up at the crackin' ceilings or around at the rats and cockroaches. What's a man to do? Cheat on your already beaten-down wife? Ignore your child? Drink until you can't stand up? Hate your mother and your sister...? Is that what a man does, Daddy? You left me with a mark, the mark of the dreamer! Don't you know that being a dreamer is dangerous? Don't you know that you can lose respect for yourself; and don't you know that it's scary and lonely?

Walter hits his Tragic Flaw repeatedly.

WALTER: I'm mad 'cause you didn't show me how to get out in the world and do things. But it's not that, Daddy. For me, you had so much to give—so much—and it didn't go nowhere but into the bottle. Daddy, tell me I ain't going that way—that my son ain't going that way.

The fear that his father's legacy will pass down to Walter's son really pops.

WALTER: Give me a sign that dreams can come true—ain't no matter if you're black in America. Tell me that I will piss

TRUTH

in my own toilet and my mother and wife will only clean up after themselves, not white folks! Take the curse of the dreamer off me! Take it off so I can be a man and live my life. Take it off so my son no longer sleeps on the living room sofa! Please, Daddy, please... Give us something other than the pain, the hurting, the liquor, the bigotry... Give us a new legacy! If you do, I'll try to remember only the good things, Daddy. I will! All the special things you did and things you made out of nothing. Not the lying and the drinking and breaking Mama's heart. I promise, Daddy...

Walter Lee's Phone Call was solidly rooted in his *Need*, *Public Persona*, and *Tragic Flaw*. He implores his father for some kind of acknowledgment or respect at the same time that he runs himself down. His "good boy" *Public Persona* takes a back seat to the rage and frustration he feels at his inability to fulfill his dreams. His *Tragic Flaw* leaves him helplessly trying to make a bargain with a man who was as unable to help Walter achieve his ambitions in life as he is in death.

What the actor has to say in the Phone Call is very personal. So personal, in fact, that some actors balk at following through on the Phone Call exercise. Inevitably, there are those who'll say, "They hung up on me," or "I would never talk to my father (or mother, or stepsister, or ex-husband) that way," or "They're not listening, they never did listen," or any of a million other excuses. To resist the Phone Call is to resist the joy of the imagination. You're finally saying everything you've always wanted and needed to say, but without any risk. By giving yourself permission to expose true feeling, you experience the power of the imagination.

Remember the comic impersonator Peter Von Sellers? Over the course of the first few weeks of classes, I discover that Peter is genuinely gifted, and is capable of going far beyond mere imitation. He was fearless on his Journey of the Need. I can't wait to see what he does for his Fourth Wall Phone Call.

As Peter's Phone Call exercise begins, he's sitting with his feet up on a desk. Even though it's January in New York, he changed into a skimpy pair of running shoes for the exercise. Before picking up the phone, Peter slowly sucks on a banana. No one in the class eyen snickers—frankly, we're all afraid to move.

Finally, Peter picks up the phone.

"Hello, Dad? Yes...Guess what? No, I didn't get an acting job... C'mon, guess! No... Well, remember how you used to always say faggot this and faggot that?"

He pauses to devour the banana.

"Yes, you did. Not godfathering, Dad... Guess what? I'm a homosexual! Homo-sexual. No, Dad, God and I are fine. Pray for yourself. God may have questions about homosexuality—but he don't like ugliness, and you're an ugly bigot."

It's clear from Peter's expression that his father has hung up on him. Peter calls him back.

"Don't do that again! Yes, I am telling you what to do. I can because I'm calling from a world in which I am free to

explore all possibilities. I can even say that I love you. Yes, Dad, I love you. I don't want to lose you."

Peter starts to cry. You could hear a pin drop in the studio. He smiles through the tears.

"That felt good. I got to cry without you punching me or calling me a faggot. Dad? No, Dad, don't cry, I'm here. We'll talk. It's okay, but guilt isn't going to do either of us any good. No, don't feel sorry for me, I can use it, thank God. Yes, thank God! But you, what will you do with it, Dad? You have to use it, create with it somehow; otherwise, you'll never change, and you'll always be an ugly bigot! I hate and I love you. I want to kill you, and I want to rescue you. I can play Stanley or Blanche! Most of all, I love you, Dad. And I don't want to lose you now that I finally know who I am. Dad, I fell in love. I fell in love, and I don't want to lose him either!"

Peter cries again as he hangs up the phone. His honest and moving emotional roller-coaster ride is over.

SUSAN BATSON

CHAPTER THIRTEEN

OBJECTS:
LOST AND FOUND

Rejoice with me, for I have found my sheep, which was lost.

Luke 15:6

INSIDE THE BOX

Forrest Gump was a huge box-office hit. It took the Best Picture, Best Actor, and Best Director Oscars in the 1994 Academy Awards. But I can only remember one thing from it—a box of chocolates. Everything else, for me, in *Forrest Gump* is a blur.

There was something about the way that Forrest held the box, something about how lovingly he cradled it in his lap, and the way he kept his hands on it, that was far more eloquent to me than anything he said about it. Life may be like a box of chocolates; but in Tom Hanks's hands, Forrest's box carried much more than just metaphor. The box of chocolates carried *Need*.

Forrest caresses and cherishes that chocolate box as a physical reminder of his childhood. Forrest's mother patiently protected him. She taught him how to live beyond the limits of his leg braces and his below-average intelligence. "I'm not a smart man," Forrest later tells his lifelong unrequited love, Jenny, "but I know what love is." He knows what love is because his mother taught him.

I believe Forrest's box of chocolates carried something equally strong for Forrest the character and Tom Hanks the actor. In the scenes with the box, something from Hanks's own childhood percolated in him. Consciously or unconsciously, Hanks *endowed* that box with his own *Need* "to be mothered."

I've never met Tom Hanks, and have never worked with him. I don't know what preparation went into his performance. But I do know that I'll never forget that box. I won't forget it because it was endowed with a *Need*.

Great actors bring objects and props to life just as they bring characters to life. Does anyone remember anything about *The Caine Mutiny* more vividly than Humphrey Bogart's obsessive cradling of a few steel bearings when his character has taken the stand? Think of the way John Voight swings his fringed jacket around and adjusts his hat in *Midnight Cowboy*; or how Robert De Niro, in *Taxi Driver*, dry-fires a gun into his mirror. Winona Ryder and Jessica Lange both handled their characters' diaries as if they were parts of themselves in *Girl Interrupted* and *Frances*. In these actors' hands, the objects themselves carry *Need* as much as their characters.

SUSAN BATSON

SEEK AND YE SHALL FIND

To learn how to endow an object with the energy and necessity of *Need*, I have actors do an exercise called Lost and Found. For example, I would ask your actor to choose an object. It should be something that you can easily imagine having to find in a hurry if it were lost. Then would I ask you to build a simple scenario around losing that object.

The rent is due, but the checkbook's missing. A relative is ill and in the hospital, but the car keys can't be found. The flight leaves in an hour; where are the plane tickets? Whatever the scenario, it must be both compelling and simple enough to sustain a five-minute search for that object.

But beneath the practical circumstances of their search, actors must endow the missing object with their *Need*, using their own personal material—what they uncovered in their *Journey of the Need*—to bring a *Need* of their own to their search. The actor commits to that *Need* and to the belief that finding the missing object will fulfill it.

A checkbook might carry the *Need* "to be safe." The car keys could bear the *Need* "to be mothered." The plane ticket has the *Need* "to be free." The story arc of this exercise—knowing what object is missing, why it's vital to find it, and the *Need* that you've chosen to endow it with—is important. But the object of the exercise isn't just to tell the story.

When Lost and Found is done well, the actor spontaneously creates truthful behavior as the scenario unfolds. Not the general, unfocused behavior of a hypothetical situation, but the very real behavior of a person who has lost something and responds to the search for it with *Need*.

So many of the actors I've worked with over the years have used lost money as their Lost and Found object. Actor Walter Lee, for instance, might choose to search for where his mother has hidden the insurance check that Walter has earmarked for his liquor store purchase.

I'd ask Walter the actor to take a slip of paper that will represent a check and hide it in the family apartment set he has set up in the studio. When the exercise begins, he has five minutes in which to search for that check as if it's lost. Walter would concentrate on endowing the missing check with the *Need* "to be respected." He must believe, for his five-minute search, that until he finds that object he will not be able to have his *Need* fulfilled.

What makes Walter's search real, rather than merely marking five minutes of time before miraculously pulling the check out of its hiding place in the top drawer of his mother's bureau, is his *Need*. With the check missing, he has no chance of being respected. It's an emotional sensation he knows all too well: one that his imagination will lift into belief.

When an actor like Walter commits to the scenario and carries a strong sensation of his *Need* into the exercise, an interesting thing happens. As he searches, his behavior begins to mirror each of the steps of the *Journey of the Need*.

In that first moment, Walter realizes he doesn't have the check. He *drops in* to the *Need*, feeling the respect he craves moving out of his reach as he thinks about where his mother may have hidden the check. As Walter begins to search, the immediate surroundings seem to grow enormous in his eyes. What was a moment ago an ordinary room now has the emotional size and gravity of the Unfulfilled Place of the *Need*.

Next, denial sets in. Searching in the wrong spots, stumbling around, and overturning and upsetting everything around him, Walter participates in his *Need* going unfulfilled. He curses his mother for hiding the check, and his father for having started the whole thing in the first place.

Then his search takes on a more desperate tone. Walter slips into *Tragic Flaw* and sinks momentarily into helplessness. He throws up his hands in disgust, feeling helpless and victimized, perhaps demanding to know who or what is conspiring against him, and blaming everyone but himself for this predicament.

Walter's self-defeating behavior grows more infantile. There's nowhere for him to go but back to his inner child. Centered now in that child, Walter can find a way to reach out of himself. He might evoke some positive words from a person who has fulfilled his *Need* in the past. His self-respect renewed, Walter finds the check, seemingly by accident. With the object found, his *Need* "to be respected" is fulfilled.

CHAPTER FOURTEEN

THE PRIVATE MOMENT

In privacy and silence let us compensate ourselves for that cruel chastity we are obliged to display in public.
Marquis de Sade

ONE MAN SHOW

All of the major characters in *American Beauty* have at least one scene in which they are alone or they believe themselves to be alone. Lester Burnham struggles with his self-esteem as he examines himself in a mirror. Lester's wife, Carolyn, anxiously repeats a self-psyching mantra of "I will sell this house" before a client's arrival. Lester and Carolyn's daughter, Jane, searches her own bedroom mirror for an identity she can live with. Each of these scenes vividly reveals something deeply personal and private about the character in it.

The actors playing these roles have meticulously prepared and rehearsed their parts. They are performing their roles in front of scores of technicians. Nevertheless, during those solo scenes the characters Lester, Carolyn, and Jane appear to behave spontaneously. It's as if they really are by themselves, behaving so privately that the viewer feels almost like a voyeur. What Kevin Spacey, Annette Bening, and Thora Birch achieve in those moments in *American Beauty* is what Stanislavski called "public solitude."

PUBLIC PRIVACY

Stanislavski observed that, in the truest performances, the actor creates the illusion that the character is alone and unobserved, being *private in public*. Lee Strasberg was particularly inspired by Stanislavski's concept of public solitude—so much so that he developed an exercise that would prepare and accustom the actor to being private in public. Strasberg called his invention the "Private Moment."

The setup for Strasberg's Private Moment exercise was relatively simple. Each actor would identify and select an activity from real life that we would never do if we knew we were being observed. We used our imagination and recall of detail to recreate in the Actor's Studio the private place where we would do this activity. Then we would perform that activity just as if we were in our own private place.

Strasberg's actors would dance alone. We'd talk to ourselves, and sing horribly out of tune as if we were in our living rooms. We'd pick our teeth or pluck our eyebrows inside the sensorial ring of our apartment bathrooms. We would pray, cry, or laugh maniacally in hallways that we could see and anyone watching could feel. Exposing ourselves this way, we learned to peel off the layers of inhibition and self-consciousness that would keep us from being private (truthfully intimate) in public (onstage or in front of a camera).

In my opinion, the Private Moment was Lee Strasberg's greatest contribution to acting. It was also his most controversial exercise. Because as actors, we revealed our privacy in the studio, where we were observed by others, the Private Moment was often mistaken for a performance. The best Private Moments— the ones in which the actor achieved true public solitude—were very discomforting to watch. Seen as performance, a Private Moment seems like a self-indulgent, tasteless display—with way too much personal information for a complete stranger to absorb.

But the Private Moment is never a performance. It's an *EXERCISE*. Strasberg created it to strengthen the actor's abilities, not to tell a story or to communicate anything to anyone. A Private Moment should be embarrassing to watch. That's the whole point. The actor who settles for anything less hasn't achieved true privacy.

Strasberg's critics also claimed that the Private Moment was potentially dangerous. Some people saw it as an unsupervised, unrestrained psychodrama that might bring down a fragile artist's personality like a house of cards. This interpretation was utter nonsense. Strasberg carefully screened actors. He let us all know that the exercise was exploratory work, not self-interrogation, exhibitionism, or a confession of any kind.

When I first learned about the Private Moment, it was clear to me how safe it was; for I realized that I'd been doing Private Moments for years.

BEHIND CLOSED DOORS

As a kid, I had a ritual game I used to play in secret inside the bathroom of my family's home. In the bathroom mirror, I transformed into a famous and sexy blues singer. I wasn't interested in Motown like my sisters and the other kids my age. Instead of pretending to be Diana Ross, I became Ella Fitzgerald or Dinah Washington or Billy Holiday.

I also made believe, with a kid's absolute faith, that I had a band backing me up. They were all guys who I knew or regularly encountered in the neighborhood. I pretended they were the musicians in my band. We rehearsed together for hours on end, those guys and I. It was my group! I was the boss, and I called the tune. I had their full attention. Every time I snapped my fingers, I imagined the guys in the band following the tempo I set. I made sure they were watching my every move.

I would have been mortified if anyone saw me doing my singer routine. I went out of my way to be sure that no one would discover me talking to people who weren't actually there, and singing into a toothbrush that was my microphone.

The sexy torch singer game was my little-kid way of exploring what I understood about men's attention. I didn't know how to deal with being sexual at that age. Though my mother was very upfront about sex and biology, we didn't really communicate about the feelings and attitudes behind the birds and the bees. In those moments alone in the bathroom, I was working out a fear. I needed my mother to help me to understand and to handle the male-female thing. I felt afraid, and I needed her guidance.

SUSAN BATSON

As we get older, we get more self-conscious. But we continue to have solitary times in our lives. If we were observed in some of these moments, we'd be giving more away about our true selves than we ever would dare if we knew we were being watched. Our behavior during these times is private because it is unfiltered. There's no mask of *Public Persona* between our *Need* and the world.

That was part of the genius of Strasberg's invention. An actor doing the Private Moment exercise succeeds when he *drops in* to a *Need*. When a Private Moment really cooks, when the actor really achieves Stanislavski's public solitude, the actor is in the *Need*, really experiencing the *Need's* energy. There's no chance of any audience intruding on the actor's privacy.

I'd gone to charm school. I'd been in children's theater. I had a whole bag of musical theater tricks when I came to the Actor's Studio. The Private Moment taught me that those things were elements of my *Public Persona*, not of any *Need*. They gave me confidence, but they didn't necessarily give me truth. If I wanted to really exist in the intimate reality of a character's *Need*, I had to be able to expose and explore a *Need* of my own.

THE PERSONAL PRIVATE MOMENT

It's important to remember that much of Strasberg's most brilliant work was done during an era when Lenny Bruce went to jail for telling dirty jokes. Mindful of the witch-hunt mentality of the time, Strasberg held back on the truly private nature of his Private Moment exercise. He sometimes allowed actors to use behavior that was as much habitual as it was truly personal. I've retooled Strasberg's brilliant discovery with the *Need* in mind. I call it the Personal Private Moment.

The way to the *Need* is through the actor's own intimacy. Since intimacy is what we're after, in the Personal Private Moment, I ask the actor to use the most intimate behavior that comes to mind. Anything short of masturbation or going to the toilet is fair game.

In Personal Private Moments I've seen, *Needs* vividly exposed as actors tenderly kissed themselves in their bathroom mirrors, or frantically played air guitar in their bedrooms as if they were in a stadium. I've had male actors dress themselves in women's clothing. I've seen actors talk to God, and apparently hear God talk back. I've seen the abyss of loneliness and disconnection scream out as an actor examines family pictures in a photo album. These activities each served to untether these actors from inhibition and self-consciousness to *drop in* to *Need*.

I also ask actors to do their Personal Private Moment in front of an entire class of their fellow actors, which really tests their ability to create and maintain the sensation of the place in which they perform their private activities. They have to really put up their Fourth Wall and make their environment real for themselves. It also dares the actor to not perform. It's a tremendous challenge for the actor to achieve genuine privacy while being scrutinized by an "audience."

I ask the actors to prepare three private activities for their Personal Private Moment. If actors can't achieve public solitude and *drop in* to their *Need* in their first private activity, they go on to the second. If that isn't strong enough for them, they go on to the third. One of the three activities should release them into privacy, letting them *drop in* to their *Need*.

"Actor" Walter Lee might have a difficult time coming up with three private activities. Walter spent his entire life in the same crowded apartment. He didn't grow up fantasizing in the bathroom like I did, because his family shared a bathroom with the rest of the apartments on their floor.

But there must have been times when everyone was out of the house. With his mother at church, his wife at work, and his sister and son at school, Walter would probably have relished the chance to use what little privacy he had. Maybe he would hold a conversation with a fellow entrepreneur he imagined was his equal. Perhaps he would talk about his bright prospects with an imaginary John D. Rockefeller.

If that didn't drop Walter in to his *Need* "to be respected," and into private solitude, he'd have to try something else. Maybe Walter would give a reporter a tour of the latest liquor store in his hugely successful chain. Frankly, I think he'd have to go deeper to really *drop in* to his *Need*.

I raised my son Carl in our duplex on the Upper West Side. It wasn't a '50s South Side of Chicago tenement, by any means. But there wasn't all that much privacy in our apartment, either.

Sometimes the sound of a basketball game would come up from downstairs. I'd hear the players, the dribbling ball, the cheering crowd, the shot clock, and think nothing of it. I'd lean over the banister and catch Carl in the act of acting out the entire game himself. What I thought was the TV would turn out to be my son making the crowd noises, doing the moves, being Michael Jordan working an imaginary ball to the basket.

TRUTH

Buoyed by his kid's imagination, he made the game happen himself.

That's what I'd suggest to Walter Lee as a really potent private activity. Walter was a child of the '30s. He must have followed boxer Joe Louis, the Michael Jordan of his day. I imagine that in a Personal Private Moment, Walter would play out one of Joe Lewis's fights the way my son played at a Michael Jordan basketball game.

In his Personal Private Moment, Walter Lee would recreate Joe Louis's triumphant rematch against German boxer Max Schmeling. The Nazi propaganda machine toured Louis's 1936 loss to Schmeling as an Aryan triumph over the inferior American Negro. Facing Schmeling the second time, Louis was fighting for his country. He'd become white America's black champion.

As Walter Lee acted out Louis's 124-second defeat of Schmeling, he'd throw Louis's combination punches. He'd remember not to drop his left the way Louis had when he lost in '36. But he would also remember—amongst the cheers—the insults from racist white boxing fans that dogged Joe Louis throughout his whole career. If Walter Lee *dropped in* to his raw *Need* "to be respected," he would experience the mixed feelings behind Louis's victory over Schmeling.

Let's look at Angelina La Monroe from our circle. As her Personal Private Moment begins, she is standing naked in front of the class. It's clear from the way her eyes search a spot in front of her that she's cocooned behind a Fourth Wall imaginary mirror. She reveals a razor blade in her left hand. The class gasps as she brings the razor to her naked thigh. I almost stop the exercise, but I notice that the edge of the razor blade has been carefully blunted with Scotch tape. Angelina repeatedly slashes at her thigh. Each stroke brings her deeper into her intimacy. The sensation is real for her, and her openness pulls us in with her. She's using self-mutilation to communicate what she's unable to say in words. As she slashes at herself more and more viciously, her childhood gets released. The Private Moment becomes intolerable to watch, and I stop the exercise. I'm grateful that we didn't have to find out what her other private activities were. Her first choice worked perfectly. I'm delighted with the authenticity of Angelina's work. It was harrowing, and it was supposed to be.

PART

III

THE CHARACTER

CHAPTER FIFTEEN

THE CHARACTER HISTORY

There is properly no history, only biography.
Ralph Waldo Emerson

LACK OF JUDGMENT

"Actors are responsible to the people we play," Phillip Seymour Hoffman says. "You ultimately have to love who you're playing." That love is absolute and unconditional. And unconditional love leaves no room for judgment.

According to Denzel Washington, Alonzo Harris, the Machiavellian heavy he played in *Training Day*, is "an arrogant thief, liar, killer, and egomaniac," and "a sick, sick man who has no heart." But these words, used to describe Harris in press interviews, are words of love from Washington. There's not a moment in *Training Day* where Denzel Washington judges

Alonzo Harris. He found compassion for, in his words, "Harris the man, not Harris the cop." Through every word and with every move, Washington grounded Alonzo Harris in the sensations of the environment that corrupted him. "It takes a wolf to catch a wolf," Harris tells his rookie partner. "You gotta see the streets, you gotta smell it, you gotta taste the streets."

After *Training Day* was released, and Denzel won his Oscar, there was talk in the press about how, in *Training Day*, Washington finally played a bad guy. But Denzel invested Harris with the same humanity and gravitas as any of the gallery of righteous but flawed heroes he had played before *Training Day*. Harris's righteousness is perverse, and his flaws are bone deep.

IN COLD BLOOD

Phillip Seymour Hoffman began creating his Oscar-winning portrayal of Truman Capote in *Capote* with a mountain of research. Always a meticulous preparer of roles, Hoffman devoted months to devouring Capote's writing and to meeting friends and colleagues willing to share what they recalled of Capote's life and work. Hoffman studied the Maysles brothers' 1966 documentary *A Visit with Truman Capote*, films of Capote doing readings in New York, and the real Capote's various TV and movie appearances.

Hoffman shed forty pounds in order to better physically resemble the diminutive writer, an incredibly difficult task in itself. But the surface details of one of the most recognizable literary celebrities of the '60s and '70s could take Hoffman only so far. In fact, Phillip Seymour Hoffman has confessed that playing Truman Capote was far more than a practical technical challenge for him. He struggled with the role for much of the film's tight shooting schedule. Despite working with close friends and wonderful actors, Hoffman says that *Capote's* production was one of the most difficult times in his life.

Phillip Seymour Hoffman is a father, an advocate on behalf of his theater company, and a supporter of political causes. He has successfully turned his back on the acting fast lane. Truman Capote was promiscuous, a blithe manipulator of others, and supremely self-destructive. He died at age fifty-nine of liver failure brought on by decades of what a coroner's report described as "multiple drug intoxication."

To bring Truman Capote to actual living, breathing life with the vividness that he did, Phillip Seymour Hoffman had to be willing to examine or revisit the darkest places within himself. Unchecked ambition, sexual identity, addictive behavior: these are the kinds of things most people don't relish sorting through. Over the course of shooting, Hoffman was able to break through his resistance. "It wasn't just imitation," Hoffman has said in interviews, "it wasn't just mimicry; it was creating a character." Hoffman's act of creation required that he, in his words, "give himself over" to Truman. Ultimately, that's precisely what he did.

Hoffman crafted a performance that captured that iconic *Public Persona* of an unapologetically gay man in an intolerant era. He unearthed the profound *Need* "to be accepted" and the excruciating self-loathing that was the *Tragic Flaw* that kept Capote on a path of self-destruction leading to an early grave. By baring his own soul, Hoffman gave the character of Truman a soul.

THE LESSON OF HISTORIES

By now, you should understand what a vital creative resource the truth of the actor's own life experience is. *Need*, *Public Persona*, and *Tragic Flaw* are the bedrock of a fictional character's dramatic life, and the foundation of the actor's own life. These three forces define scripted characters because they are the same forces at work in real-life human behavior.

All characters are shaped by the circumstances set forth in a script. Many of those defining circumstances have formed long before the script's story begins. All of the characters inside a script's finite story world have a life and a history that stretches out behind them. The viewer doesn't have to see the defining moments of a character's history take place. An audience doesn't need to know the precise events behind a character's *Need*, *Public Persona*, and *Tragic Flaw*. But the actor portraying that character *does*.

Every character has a history, and the actor is responsible for knowing that history. Whether or not a character is based on a real person with a researchable biography, it's every actor's job to know the character's history as well as Philip Seymour Hoffman knew Truman Capote's biography. It makes no difference if the actor is a day player on *Law & Order* with a single line of dialogue, or in a one-man show playing Abraham Lincoln. Finding, establishing, and maintaining parallels between the actor's interior world and the character's interior world demand that the actor know everything there is to know about the character.

Ultimately the actor's job is to communicate a story. For the time being, however, our character work will not be concerned with that responsibility. To better understand the dynamic that joins a character's history to an actor's history, we'll look at characters outside the world of the script. Over the next several chapters, we'll specifically focus on uniting the truth of the actor with the truth of a character.

To do that, we'll use an historical personality, not a fictional character—which doesn't mean Truman Capote from *Capote*, or Tina Turner from *What's Love Got to Do With It*. Neither film was a documentary. Both characters were based on real people and were written using careful and thorough research. But writers reinvented Truman and Tina as characters on their own very different story journeys. Those characters were in turn interpreted as characters by Hoffman and Angela Bassett from their respective scripts, not just from the facts of the real Truman's and Tina's lives.

In order to better understand the role of research and the process by which an actor connects with a role, we'll look at "characters" liberated from a story. We'll use the real people who are defined only by the history of their own lives. These real "characters" will be our training wheels for the scripted characters to come. They are a midway point between the previous section's focus on the actor, and the next section's attention to the script text itself.

Historians and biographers tend to revise or reevaluate the personalities and lives of historical characters. Current opinions on Abraham Lincoln's personality run from historian Joshua Wolf Schenk's and novelist Gore Vidal's emphasis on Lincoln's depressive nature to Doris Kearns Goodwin's and David

Herbert Donald's portraits of Lincoln as a keen and sensitive judge of human nature. Author C. A. Tripp asserts that Abraham Lincoln's marriages were shams, and that the sixteenth president was a closeted homosexual.

To an actor exploring the character of Abraham Lincoln, any of these interpretations may be relevant. It depends on the actor's instincts. While doing research, actors must feel around and dig as deeply into the life and facts of the characters as the actors have dug in themselves through their *Journey of the Need*. If you read up exhaustively on Lincoln, Michael Jackson, Josephine Baker, Margaret Bourke-White, Kurt Cobain, Donald Trump, or Marie Antoinette, personal connections will become clear. Once enough facts have been excavated, creation begins.

"YOU MAY DO THAT"

Actors cannot judge history's heroes and villains any more than they would judge a scripted character, a next-door neighbor, a sister, or a brother. Yes, Adolf Hitler was a monster whose appalling crimes are infamous and unconscionable. But in researching Hitler the character, it would be dishonest not to acknowledge the constant physical abuse and complete absence of nurturing love of any kind that characterized Hitler's childhood. *The Public Persona* of Der Fuhrer, protector and savior of Germany, that Hitler so effectively cultivated, reflects how bottomless and unfulfillable his *Need* "to be protected" was. It in no way mitigates or trivializes his monstrous corresponding *Tragic Flaw*—sociopathic behavior.

Good deeds or bad, everyone has an unfulfilled emotional *Need*, a *Public Persona* that covers it, and a *Tragic Flaw* that erupts when *Need* and *Public Persona* jam up. No matter how much good they've done; no matter how graceful, steadfast, or incorruptible they may seem, everyone has those same three dimensions of character at work within them.

Rosa Parks was famous for refusing to give up her seat to a white man on a segregated Montgomery, Alabama city bus in 1955. Her act of defiance and subsequent arrest made the world aware of the American civil rights movement. They sparked a successful boycott of the Montgomery bus system by African-American bus riders. It was the Montgomery boycott that first placed Dr. Martin Luther King Jr. in the public eye. The boycott eventually led to the repeal of Alabama's segregation laws.

The story of the demure, God-fearing seamstress who wouldn't bend to the racist will of segregationist Alabama is the stuff of legend. In 1989, when news cameras broadcast the image of a lone protester facing down a Chinese Army tank in Tiananmen Square, Nelson Mandela declared it a "Rosa Parks moment."

Popular history recalls Rosa Parks as an angelic martyr. Her contemporaries agree with that assessment. "There was a strange religious glow about Rosa," the Congress of Racial Equality's James Farmer recalled, "a kind of humming Christian light, which gave her unique majesty." When Rosa Parks passed away in 2005, Michigan congressman John Conyers described how, for the twenty-three years Rosa worked for him, Conyers "treated her with deference because she was so quiet, so serene—just a very special person."

TRUTH

But Rosa Parks was a flesh-and-blood woman. Her long life was scarred with much pain and hardship. She was born in Tuskegee, Alabama. But when her carpenter father abandoned Rosa's mother, Leona Edwards, and their two infant children, Leona moved into a dirt-floor shack with her parents in Pine Level, Alabama.

Throughout her early childhood, Rosa was small for her age, and was plagued by colds and tonsillitis. She was left in her grandparents' care in Pine Level while her mother taught school in another town. Despite her age, size, and frailty, Rosa worked in the cotton fields like other sharecropper children, and looked after her younger bother Sylvester.

The two earliest memories she recalls in her autobiography, *Rosa Parks: My Story*, are telling. The first is receiving lavish praise from her grandfather for being well behaved. Like many children raised primarily by their grandparents, she was expected to act like an adult, even as a child. The second memory she cites is trying to fall asleep while her grandfather sat in a rocking chair nearby, holding a shotgun in his lap in case the KKK attacked their home. Little wonder she remained a lifelong insomniac.

Rosa looked after her brother when they were children, then her ailing grandmother, her alcoholic husband Raymond Parks, and her mother Leona when she fell ill. Rosa would spend her entire life taking care of others. The saintly image that both history and those who knew Rosa Parks recall is her *Public Persona*—a saint/caregiver.

Expected to grow up quickly, living without a father, and burdened by the frailties of others her whole life, the *Need* that

Rosa Parks's *Public Persona* covered was "to be taken care of" herself. One of Rosa's favorite pieces of scripture, Psalm 27, reads in part:

> *For in the time of trouble*
> *He shall hide me in His pavilion;*
> *In the secret of his tabernacle shall he hide me;*
> *He shall set me up upon a rock.*

Her lifelong devotion to the church, the sense of faith and belonging that it gave her, was a balm for that *Need*.

The completely false cliché, proliferated by the white press at the time of the boycott, is of Rosa Parks, the little Negro seamstress, who inadvertently changed American history because she was too tired to give up her seat on a bus. By the time of her arrest in 1955, Rosa had been active in the civil rights movement in Alabama for twelve years as secretary to NAACP president Edgar Nixon. She was a member of the Voter's League, and had been a vigorous activist on behalf of the Scottsboro boys and other victims of segregationist injustice.

But Rosa's civil rights work was always behind the scenes. She organized meetings, took notes, and made calls. She had never participated in actual civil disobedience. Rosa Parks's *Tragic Flaw*, the jam-up of her *Need* "to be taken care of," and her *Public Persona* of caregiver, was anger. The fact that she so rarely succumbed to that flaw in her public life has become part of her historical mystique.

And in the case of her fateful bus ride, anger made her part of history. When Rosa Parks boarded that bus in December of 1955, she was tired and fed up. Passive resistance met passive aggressiveness when she was confronted by the same bus driver who had ejected her from a Montgomery bus twelve years earlier. She was tired, sure. But when she recognized that the armed white bus driver menacing her was the same one who had ejected her from a bus twelve years earlier, she dug in her heels.

To absorb Rosa Parks the character, you, the actor, would have to know all these things and more. Armed with Rosa's *Need*, *Public Persona*, and *Tragic Flaw*, you would begin to discover and chart the important events, the physical details, and the people that defined Rosa Parks's life. You would have to read not only Rosa's memoirs, but also Douglas Brinkley's biography of her, antisegregationist Virginia Dorr's memoirs describing her friendship with Parks, and many other books.

Rosa Parks grew up in a racist, Jim Crow Alabama. At age six, Rosa remembers in her autobiography, "I was old enough to realize that we were actually not free. The Ku Klux Klan was riding through the black community, burning churches, beating up people, killing people."

From the age when she could read, she devoured any book she could find. Like many southern blacks of the era, Rosa read *Up From Slavery* and Booker T. Washington's other consciousness-raising self-help books. Reading and the realities of day-to-day survival in a racist community developed a kind of pragmatism in her. "I do not like to form in my mind an idea that I don't have any proof of," she wrote years later.

SUSAN BATSON

Rosa was a dedicated churchgoer. She read the Bible voraciously, underlining, notating, and committing passages to memory. "God is everything to me," she would say. Founded by freed slaves, the African Methodist Episcopal Church, "with its musical rhythms and echoes of Africa," Rosa wrote years later, "thrilled me when I was young."

The sensory details of Rosa's life—her inability to swallow without pain as a child, the chronic bursitis that plagued her seamstress career—would have to be explored. The taste of the salt ham, the greens, and the fried catfish of her childhood, and the pride and pleasure she recalled in "enjoying the smell of bacon frying and coffee brewing and knowing that white folks were doing the preparing instead of me," when she was a guest of the Highlander Folk School a few months before the boycott, are equally vital.

The actor taking on Rosa Parks would have to listen to the gospel music Rosa adored, read the scriptures Rosa fed off of, and look at as much of the newspaper coverage, journals, and magazines of the day as a voracious reader like Rosa Parks would consume.

In short, every recorded detail of this woman's life would have to be uncovered, and every possible connection would have to be identified. You, the actor playing Rosa Parks, would leave no stone unturned in either yourself or the character. For every important person in Rosa's life, you would create a Personalization. For every circumstance you learn about Rosa Parks, there is a possible parallel sensation from your own experience.

It's the same for any character, scripted or otherwise. It may seem like a lot of work, because it is. But, like the interior work one's actor does on oneself, it pays off. The details, facts, and trivia of history are potent raw materials for creating a character. As story guru Robert McKee (who, not coincidentally, began his career as an actor) writes in his book "Story," "We landscape character biographies, planting them with events that become a garden we'll harvest again and again."

CHAPTER SIXTEEN

THE CHARACTER PRIVATE MOMENT

You have at least 75 percent in common with any character
you play, whether it's Hitler or Peter Pan.
You couldn't lose it if you wanted to.
Jack Nicholson

PRIVATE LIVES

The Personal Private Moment is a wonderful conditioning tool that helps accustom the actor to accessing the actor's own intimacy. The actor who learns to achieve public solitude via the Personal Private Moment has made a tremendous step towards harnessing the intimacy required to create a character. But the Private Moment itself is not just a way for the actor to explore the actor's own intimacy. It can also be used to explore the intimacy of the character.

The scenes in *American Beauty* of Lester, Carolyn, and Jane Burnham unself-consciously revealing themselves; the moments in *Midnight Cowboy* and *Taxi Driver* in which Joe Buck and Travis Bickle talk to their mirrors, all catch these characters in revealing Private Moments. In these scenes, these characters unself-consciously reveal themselves at a level of intimacy that's almost uncomfortable. For an actor to get down into the character with that same intensity of intimacy, I recommend exploration through a Character Private Moment. Through the Character Private Moment, actors can incorporate their own intimacy within the intimacy of their character.

The Character Private Moment asks actors to filter their intimacies through the facts and history they know of the character. To begin, the actors choose a place in which, according to their research, the character would be truly private. Once again, actors' responsibility is to the facts. They must not only decide where and what the place is, but what's in it, what sensory details it might possess. Is it hot? Is it cold? What's the light like? How does it smell? What does it sound like?

Then, so that the actor can imbue the character with the actor's own truthful intimacy, the actor chooses three private activities. Like the Personal Private Moment, these activities have to involve behavior the actor personally knows well, but would never do in public.

The Character Private Moment unites:

1. **The character's circumstances: the facts defining the Private Moment scenario.**
2. **The actor's intimacy: three private activities the actor would never perform in public.**

In the Character Private Moment, the actor blends the character's life and the actor's *sensation*—the gut experience of emotional and physical reality—using imagination. Through the imagination, the actor combines the truth of the actor's own intimacy with the intimacy of the character. When a Character Private Moment is done well, the actor gets valuable firsthand knowledge and experience with the character's inner life. The actor also opens up to personal revelations and epiphanies about the character that can be used as choices in an actual performance.

I've seen the Character Private Moment work miracles this way. As actors find a commonality between themselves and their roles, judgment vanishes, and performances take on a feeling of actual life.

ROSA PARKS: CHARACTER PRIVATE MOMENT

From research, I know that Rosa Parks was so pious that she wouldn't even dance outside of Church. She was married to a very handsome man. He drank and she didn't. Rosa remained childless her entire life. Her *Public Persona* is virtually devoid of any sexuality.

Would she explore her sensual and sexual nature in private? An actor exploring Rosa Parks might want to do something like my childhood torch singer routine—one where I'm a sexy performer with an all-male band. That would be a strong first personal activity—have Rosa secretly vamp and display her sexuality in her Private Moment.

Rosa was very light skinned. Research tells me that one of her great-grandparents was white—a Scotch-Irish indentured slave. It was rumored in her family that her father's grandfather may have been a white Yankee soldier. Would she wonder in private what it would be like to "pass"? Would she try out white mannerisms in her mirror? I've never regretted my heritage, but like many African-Americans, I have sometimes wondered how my life might have been different if I hadn't been born black. For an actress exploring Rosa Parks, "passing" could serve as a second personal activity.

Rosa Parks spent her entire life taking care of others. She protected her fatherless younger brother, she looked after her grandmother when she became ill, and she looked after her mother after that. She tolerated her husband's binge drinking. Wouldn't she harbor rage and frustration at being a woman of such strong inner resources and intelligence, confined to a caretaker role?

I was a single mother. I raised my son without child support or welfare. Keeping a roof over his head, keeping him clothed and fed, and getting the best education possible for him was a challenging task. I never complained about it; but during difficult times, I occasionally found myself slipping into self-pity and resentment in private. An actress with a similar parallel would actually probably enjoy releasing that anger and sharing it with Rosa.

This is research meeting speculation. We're in the realm of the imagination. Anything goes in this exercise, as long as it has the truth of intimacy. We're not putting on a show here; we're exploring character.

SUSAN BATSON

PLACE

The home of Rosa Parks—a small apartment in the Cleveland Courts projects, in Montgomery County, Alabama. It is a Saturday afternoon in early 1956. The yearlong Montgomery Bus Boycott is still only a few months old. Raymond Parks is working at his barbershop, and Rosa's mother Leona McCauley is at church, cleaning it for Sunday services. Rosa lost her job after she was arrested. She has subsisted on what tailoring work she can take between speaking engagements (for which she refuses any money) and organizing activities.

The actor exploring Rosa finishes cleaning the sparsely furnished stage representing her apartment from top to bottom. She sets down a mop with pride.

> *Rosa Parks lived with her mother and her husband in a small apartment in the Cleveland Courts projects in Montgomery. There must have been very few times when she was alone. The actor explores Public Persona of the saint/caregiver reveling in having taken care of the apartment chores.*

Rosa crosses to a full-length mirror that she uses for doing fittings for her clients. She rubs and stretches her sore right arm while looking at her reflection.

> *Rosa suffered from bursitis, a painful tissue inflammation brought on by repetitive stress, for her entire adult life. The actor has prepared using a Sense Memory of similar*

TRUTH

pain and of a fear that the toll of an illness will be too high.

Rosa Parks stops and stares at herself in the mirror. In a quiet little voice, she says, "Mirror, mirror on the wall, who's the fairest of them all?" Rosa moves close to the mirror, removes her glasses, and pulls her hair back, straightening it against her skull. It stretches her eyes until they are slightly slanted. She smiles.

Rosa's brother Sylvester was nicknamed "Chink" because of his slanted eyes. Clearly, this actor has personalized a sibling or another loved one close to her for Rosa's brother.

She studies her light skin in the mirror, and then looks down at her arm. Rosa's thoughts drift to her grandfather, whom many people mistook as white. She starts to weep—not out of longing to be white, but because of her grandfather's commitment to his black ancestry and to that identity.

Rosa Parks's light-skinned grandfather Sylvester Edwards had a profound influence on her. He was a man of tremendous dignity who took pride in his African heritage. She was also inspired by Walter White, the blond-haired, blue-eyed, mixed-ancestry African-American who established the Atlanta NAACP in 1916. The actor has successfully personalized a respected and loved older relative. She also uses the Sense Memory of an experience of bigotry or discrimination.

SUSAN BATSON

Rosa goes to her bureau and pulls a handkerchief out of the top drawer. She blows her nose, then moves to the radio and turns it on. It warms up, and she hears an *Amos and Andy* episode. She quickly tunes in to a jazz show. The pure, hot, sweet tones of Ella Fitzgerald fill the air. Rosa looks around, checking to see if anyone could be watching her. Her bursitis-ridden body releases into a soothing, swaying rhythm. She doesn't know any dance steps, but she knows how to let music seduce her. Her movements grow more and more sensual as she lets her pelvis get into action.

Her body's free, sexual movement causes Rosa to release more inhibition. She laughs. She's discovering her sexual self.

> *Rosa's friend Virginia Durr had recently introduced her to Ella's music. Rosa never danced; but her church, the African Methodist Episcopal Church, encouraged parishioners to move with the gospel music and hymns in their services. I get a sensation of the sexual allure of Ella Fitzgerald's music. The actress uses a Sense Memory of dancing with sexual abandon. Her daughter comes from a released sensation of joy, not a mechanical attempt to laugh. It's very real.*

With her body and spirit alive and free, she sings out with Ella, unaware of the tears streaming down her face.

Suddenly she calls out, "Thank you, God, thank you, Jesus!" Then she starts chanting, "I got my mind stayed on freedom." She rushes to the radio and turns it off. She picks up a pillow off the sofa and buries her head in it. Then she takes a pillow and beats it against the arm of the sofa.

Rosa spent her life bound to a responsibility to look after those around her. The actor has slipped from Rosa's Tragic Flaw of anger to her Need "to be taken care of."

"I'm beautiful, I'm smart, I am alive! Why can't I be free? Momma! Too much! I'm not strong! I'm not! No more! I want someone to take care of me! Momma!" Rosa's aching body collapses into the sofa, and she curls up and whimpers like a baby.

I stop the exercise. By this point continuing to watch would be truly voyeuristic. The actor's intimacy and the character's intimacy have merged. The goal of the exercise has been reached.

CHAPTER SEVENTEEN

THE CHARACTER PHONE CALL

Self-expression must pass into communication for its fulfillment
Pearl S. Buck

HELLO, IT'S ME

We've seen how an improvised phone call can help the actor to communicate the *Need* hidden underneath the actor's mask of *Public Persona*. Since any character an actor might play is just as much defined by a *Need*, *Public Persona*, and *Tragic Flaw*, there is invariably someone to whom that character would unsuccessfully go to have a *Need* fulfilled. And there is a phone call that the actor can improvise as that character that will give the actor an intimate sense of the character's *Need*.

Through the Character Phone Call, that actor puts a face on the character's *Need*. As in the actor's own phone call, the actor's own experience and *Need* provide the authentic emotion. Using his imagination, the actor transforms personal truth into art. The actor scours the character's biography and identifies a person to whom the character unsuccessfully goes to have the *Need* fulfilled. Then, through sensitive and thorough research, the actor becomes familiar with the character's relationship to that person.

From the *Journey of the Need* the actor knows the name and the face of someone to whom he's repeatedly gone to have his *Need* fulfilled unsuccessfully. He knows the moments and the sensations of that experience. From his own phone call, he also has a memory of having spoken to that person, of having successfully brought that person to life and made the person listen. In the Character Phone Call he will use that stockpile of knowledge and memory to do the same thing for his character.

Researching Rosa Parks's life, I know that her father abandoned her, her mother, and her brother when Rosa was about three. She would see him again in childhood only once, at age five, when he came to Pine Level to stay for a few days with Leona, Sylvester (then three), and little Rosa. She did not see him or speak to him again until she was grown and married. Rosa's *Need* "to be taken care of/protected" is deeply tied into her abandonment by her father. What would a phone call between Rosa Parks and James McCauley be like? What would Rosa want to say to a man who turned his back on a loving, dutiful wife and two toddlers?

A three-dimensional performance calls for three-dimensional thinking. In the Character Phone Call, your imagination should take you anywhere there is the truth of real feeling from your own life, as well as to the character's biography. Anything is fair game as long as it rings true emotionally. As Johnny Depp has said in press interviews, "To be an actor is to be something of a pirate."

Thinking about Rosa Parks and James McCauley, I remember another famous woman who was abandoned by her father. Marilyn Monroe's birth certificate bears the name Norma Jean Mortenson, after her mother's second husband Edward Mortenson. But Edward Mortenson had abandoned Marilyn and her mother before Marilyn was born. Marilyn's mother Gladys would always maintain that her actual father was a man named Stanley Gifford. Gladys and Gifford had an affair around the time of Marilyn's conception. When Marilyn was a child, her mother showed her Gifford's picture and told her, "This is your father."

Marilyn tried to contact Gifford throughout her life, but he refused to speak with her. In *After the Fall*, playwright Arthur Miller, one of Marilyn's ex-husbands, dramatized a phone call between Marilyn Monroe and Stanley Gifford. I clearly remember seeing Barbara Loden play "Maggie," Marilyn's alter ego, in *After the Fall*. Her performance was truthful and devastating.

Also, my own father died when I was very young. I have often experienced feelings of abandonment that are a hangover from my father's early death. Choosing to perform Rosa's phone call when she was forty-two, the age she was in 1955, I would think about the things I might say to my own father at that age. I would also do a Personalization of my father, recalling his strongest physical feature, strongest human quality, something he would say or do, and so on, until it triggered a sensation of my father that I could use for Rosa's father.

ROSA PARKS: CHARACTER PHONE CALL

It's spring of 1956. Rosa's mother's health is failing, and Rosa has had to put her in the hospital. Rosa and her husband Raymond are both out of work, victims of nervous white employers who want nothing to do with the boycott. For the first time in her life, Rosa finds herself in debt. Raymond is on a drinking binge. Rosa is very scared for the future and feels very alone.

Armed with these facts, armored by the truth of her own experience, her imagination popping and creative juices flowing, the actor exploring Rosa Parks takes her place on the set representing Rosa's apartment. It's time to take poetic license. Alone, Rosa dials the phone.

> ROSA: Hello... May I speak to James McCauley? Oh, you are James McCauley... Fine, thank you, and how are you, Mr. McCauley? ...I can't. I know you are my father, but I don't know you as "Daddy," so I can't call you that... Momma isn't doing well. In fact, she's in the hospital... I will... Sylvester? He lives in Detroit now. He wouldn't stay in the South, where they won't let a decorated returning veteran wear his uniform in public because of his skin color... He's married with thirteen children.
>
> *The actor should prepare a Personalization like the one I described of my father.*

ROSA: Why do you care? I mean, do you care anything about us? Why do you ask after my mother and my brother? Why haven't you picked up the phone or a pen to write us? Why? ...Don't you dare hang up on me! I will call you back, and call you back again.

I'm getting the sensation of Rosa's Tragic Flaw.

ROSA: Oh, you've heard. You've seen me in the papers and on TV? ...Yes, I am a member of the NAACP. I know you don't want to know my politics; in fact, you don't really want to know anything about me. But let me tell you, I've been doing your job for decades. I've looked after Sylvester, Grandma, Momma, everyone! I didn't even have the time to finish high school until I was a grown, married woman! And I'm a teacher's daughter! It was my husband who encouraged me to finish school, not my father! ...Do you have any idea, sir, what you've done to your wife, your children? Do you even care? I know you are a very, very godless man—there's so little goodness in you.

This example shows good, thorough researching on the actor's part. Though a lifelong bookworm and an A student, Rosa didn't finish high school until after she was married. There's more sensation of Rosa's Tragic Flaw in the growing indignation and anger in her phone call.

ROSA: No, I called you to ask for help. Momma is frail, so, so sick, and I need help. I need money, I need some peace. ...I do, I do believe in God. Without him, I don't know where I'd be. But why couldn't you be a father? We needed you. Everything became so hard for Momma and my grandparents... What a hateful thing to say! I was taught to "love your enemies, do good to them that hate you..." Yes, my people do believe in turning the other cheek. I'm trying to do this now... I NEED YOU—I NEED A FAMILY—I NEED A FATHER WHO CARES... I WANT YOU TO COME BACK AND MAKE EVERYTHING ALL RIGHT... My husband? Oh God, don't be so evil. He's not doing so good... Yes, you make yourself very clear—don't worry I won't call you again. But sir, if you need to call me, I will be there for you; but I promise you I will never call you again, James McCauley!

The actor experiences the sensation of Rosa's Need "to be taken care of."

Rosa hangs up the phone.

ROSA: "I will lift up mine eyes unto the hills, from whence cometh my help. My help cometh from the Lord, which made heaven and earth. He will not suffer thy foot to be moved: he that keepeth thee will not slumber. Behold, he that keepeth Israel shall neither slumber nor sleep. The Lord is thy keeper: the Lord is thy shade upon thy right hand. The sun shall not smite thee by day, nor the moon by night. The Lord shall preserve thee from all evil: He shall preserve thy soul. The Lord shall preserve thy going out and thy coming in from this time forth, forevermore."

Rosa often quoted from the 121st Psalm. The actor, still dropped in to the Need, uses it to express Rosa's Need one last time.

The exercise is complete. I don't have to know whom the actor was personalizing, or what personal material she accessed to prepare for the phone call. It is obvious from the way she vividly released the sensation of Rosa's *Need* and *Tragic Flaw*, and from the way that she incorporated the facts of Rosa's life, that the actor did her homework.

CHAPTER EIGHTEEN

THE ANIMAL

An actor is never so great as when he reminds you of an animal—
falling like a cat, lying like a dog, moving like a fox.
François Truffaut

TALK TO THE ANIMALS

When *Midnight Cowboy* was released in 1969, the *New York Times* review of the film singled out Dustin Hoffman's performance as Ratso Rizzo—"With his hair matted back, his ears sticking out and his runty walk," the *Times* said, "Hoffman looks like a sly, defeated rat." Ten years later, the same critic made a similar observation about Robert De Niro's Jake La Motta in *Raging Bull*. "There's not one sequence in the film," according to the *Times*, "where he hasn't behaved like an animal."

Any similarity between Hoffman's and De Niro's characters and actual animals was purely intentional. Both actors meticulously prepared their roles with those animals specifically in mind. Human beings have imitated animals, even deified them and taken them as spirit guides, since the dawn of time. And **Animal Work** has been in use in acting since Stanislavski's day. A character doesn't have to be named Ratso or be compared to a bull in the film's title to make animal behavior an appropriate tool for an actor.

The actor uses Animal Work to layer truthful and vivid life into a character. Animal Work frees you from the narrow limits of your own ordinary behavior and movement. It gives you a way to create wholly new behavior with which to define and individualize your character.

When you successfully internalize animal behavior, your audience doesn't necessarily realize it. Animal Work creates a tangible physical reality underneath the character's words and movements that, though clearly present, remains almost indefinable. The audience simply cannot take their eyes off of you. Think of the distinctive physicality the x-factor magnetism of the following performances. Each of them was prepared with these animals in mind.

Marlon Brando	Vito Corleone	*The Godfather*	Bulldog shot in the throat
Al Pacino	Sonny Wortzik	*Dog Day Afternoon*	Mutt
Robert De Niro	Max Cady	*Cape Fear*	Snake
Tom Cruise	Frank T. J. Mackey	*Magnolia*	Fox
Juliette Binoche	Rose	*Jet Lag*	Cat

For far too many contemporary actors, building a character comes down to a little makeup and a change of costume. The use of Animal Work has faded from popularity in the last few decades. Women actors are under so much Pressure to look as beautiful as possible, and remain conventionally attractive, that they rarely incorporate Animal Work into characters. Un-actor-friendly directors often don't know how to handle Animal Work. "What was *that?*" they'll ask. "I don't like the way she looks." "Does she have to be that angry?" They're more comfortable with an easy, unthreatening surface than a truthful, deep character.

It's a shame, because, when it's done responsibly, Animal Work is a very potent defense against generalized acting, and conventional, cliché behavior. It can result in a Ratso Rizzo.

But there are certain people that have been doing Animal Work their whole lives. They may not realize it, but they already are animals. The way they move, and the way they adapt to the motion of people around them, suggest that they won't resist or struggle with the Animal process itself.

ANIMUS

Most people have an animal they feel they resemble, or that they identify with to some degree. If I get a strong animal sensation from an actor when I teach Animal Work, I'll tell the actor so. Sometimes an actor's zodiac sign suggests an animal. For character Animal Work, the actor looks at the character and at himself in search of an animal that connects him with his part.

For Rosa Parks, her small stature, her quiet dignity, and the tone of her voice (on display in documentaries like *Eyes On the*

Prairie) suggest a cat. Rosa just seems catlike. Many people identify with cats and their tidy independence; so perhaps an actor exploring the character of Rosa Parks through Animal Work would respond to that connection.

Animal Work begins with research. What, the actor asks, are the irrefutable facts of my specific animal's appearance, behavior, and motion? The elephant's heavy side-to-side lope, the owl's alert scrutiny, the cheetah's bursts of speed—these are all simple, straightforward truths. Zoos, pet stores, the Discovery Channel, and Animal Planet offer ways to observe animal behavior and motion. Preparing Animal Work, you observe as much of this material as you can find. The deeper your research, and the more specific your choices, the more powerful your Animal Work will be.

You're a snake? Then you'll have to make a decision from your research about what kind of snake. Rattlesnakes, cobras, and the large constrictor snakes all have distinctive behavior. The actor filters these facts through his own instincts, and makes a choice. For Max Cady in *Cape Fear,* I imagine that Robert De Niro chose a cobra. The way De Niro displays Cady's upper body suggests a cobra's hood. When Cady savagely attacks and bites Illeana Douglas's character Lori, he drops down on her, rather than springing at her. Unlike rattlers, cobras use gravity when they bite, instead of coiled muscular movement.

To underlay Rosa the character with cat behavior, the first step is to study a cat's characteristic motion, its expressions, and the sounds it makes. Once the research is in and these details are identified and sorted out, the physical work begins.

PLAY

Playing at the animal, moving around like the animal, trying out the distinctive moves and behavior of the animal for yourself, allows your actor to discover and explore the physical life of the animal. The snake's effortless, probing movement; the lion's swaying, heavy-pawed walk; the horse's head bob; these movements are second nature to the animals. Through play, you commit to the animal's "actual" physical nature—how the real animal moves and lives.

An actor exploring Rosa/cat would have to get down on all fours, roll around on the floor, sniff the air, stretch, and do whatever it takes to experience the sensations of the cat behavior studied. Through play, the actor finds the physical sensation of the fur and the tail, the ears, the eyes, the light step, the articulate spine, and the perfect balance in the actor's own body and movements.

ADD SOUND

As that physical sensation becomes stronger, you experiment with the sounds the animal makes. De Niro incorporated a slight sibilance and tongue movement in Max Cady that's reminiscent of a snake's hissing. For Rosa Parks, an actor would experiment with the characteristic sounds that cats make. There's more to a house cat's vocalizations than just meowing, mewing, or hissing. Cats have a large vocabulary of chirps and purrs that they use to get attention or to communicate their moods or wants. The actor exploring Rosa would have to discover those things for herself while playing as a cat.

PERFORM SPECIFIC ANIMAL BEHAVIOR

Once the sound and movement flow organically, the actor performs the specific parts of the animal's behavior. The cat would stretch, groom, play, sleep, and eat through the actor's body. When challenged, cats will turn to the side in order to seem bigger. They mark territory with glands in their muzzles and their paws. An actor exploring a cat would have to try all of these things.

STAND THE ANIMAL UP

The Latin name for one of our early human ancestors is *Homo erectus*—"upright man." We are the only creatures on earth able to stand erect on two feet at all times. To humanize the animal, once the specific animal behavior has been explored, the actor must stand the animal up.

The way to do this is with the actor's spine. Tail, wings, long neck—these animals-only attributes are all fastened to the animal's spine. In Animal Work, you use your own spine to find the sensation of these features. A full-grown lion can grow to eight feet in length. Its tremendous power and grace come out of that length. To incorporate a lion into a character, you would have to use your imagination to bring the sensation of that tail and imposing length into an upright, standing position.

Cats are unusually agile and possess remarkable balance. The actor humanizing a cat for Rosa Parks would look for that centered ease and grace in her own spine. One of the strongest sensations that can serve the actor doing Animal Work is the tail.

SUSAN BATSON

Using her imagination, the actor would look for a sensation of tail and incorporate it into her own posture. The actor would be apt to hang on to that sensation when humanizing the animal. Cats also communicate moods with their tails. Rosa Parks, therefore, might exhibit subtle changes in posture and balance depending on her emotional state.

In *Cape Fear*, Robert De Niro incorporated the cobra's looming, ready-to-strike stance in Max Cady's walk. De Niro also kept his arms close to his body and his legs close together. Cady tended to stand unusually close to the characters he menaced. He even did a snake lunge at the camera while leaving prison in the opening of the film.

Cats are *digitigrades*—they primarily walk on their toes. So the humanized Rosa Parks cat would have a light, quiet gait. Having thoroughly researched Rosa Parks's life, the actor playing her would have to incorporate Rosa's chronic bursitis into the cat exploration. For a small mammal like a cat, infirmity is weakness; and weakness is potentially lethal. Experimenting with the fear and feral, defensive anger of a wounded cat would inform Rosa's *Tragic Flaw*.

The cat's front legs and paws have surprising dexterity. They can bat, swat, and grab with their paws. Cats can also manipulate objects with them. Rosa Parks was a skilled seamstress who worked with her hands constantly. Rosa's physicality is in the hooked wrists of humanized cat paws.

Standing and moving in humanized fashion, the actor now incorporates the animal through facial expressions. Max Cady has very strong snake behavior in his face. Underneath his slicked-back hair, Cady's eyes are unmoving and unblinking like a snake's. And De Niro holds Cady's mouth in fixed positions, with almost no lip movement. It gives Cady the expressionless, lipless appearance of a reptile. When he laughs, Cady's jaws yawn open in a fixed position, like a feeding snake.

A cat's mouth and face aren't as expressive as a human's. But researching Rosa Parks via documentary footage would reveal that she wasn't prone to particularly strong facial expressions herself. Finding the cat's set jaw in Rosa's sober countenance would deepen the connection between animal, actor, and character.

Your research will have told you that cats, like snakes and a few other animals, have a Jacobson's organ: a bulb of sensitive nerves hidden just behind their teeth, that supercharges the cat's sense of smell. Playing Rosa Parks, you might explore sensations based on a placid exterior, but an extremely sensitive and observant interior.

Many of Rosa Parks's contemporaries commented on how soft-spoken she was. In *Eyes On the Prize* and archived news interviews, Rosa has a smooth, easy Alabama accent. She tended to glide through vowel sounds in a purring way, and turned up the ends of sentences almost as if she were asking questions. She also had a slight sibilance in her speech that came out when she pronounced *s*'s. The actor playing her would work to layer the sensation and sound of a cat's quiet chirps and purrs, and the way that a cat's tongue forms these sounds, into Rosa's unique way of speaking.

Finally, the actor incorporates cat behavior into Rosa's behavior. As Rosa, the actor sits down with her hands folded, using the same delicacy with which a cat rests one Paw on another. She retains the cat's inquisitive, alert eye movement and mostly neutral expression. She walks silently on the balls of her feet, mirroring the cat's nimble ease. The seamstress's delicate but dexterous hands, slowed somewhat by the pain of bursitis, echo the cat's paws. She eats and drinks tidily, taking small bites and sips as a cat does.

What comes out of this process is a character that is grounded in multiple truths. The first is the truth of Rosa Parks's life: her *Need, Public Persona,* and *Tragic Flaw,* and the actual circumstances and events that shaped her. The second is the truth of the actor's own life: what you would personally bring from your own experience and emotional life to the character of Rosa. The third is the truth of imagination: what an active imagination makes of the careful study and thorough exploration of Animal Work in character.

CHAPTER NINETEEN

PLACE OF DEFEAT

Life is truly known only to those who suffer, lose,
endure adversity and stumble from defeat to defeat.
Anais Nin

"DECEPTION, DECEPTION"

Stages and movie sets require that the actor sustain unshakable faith. The audience knows immediately if the actor doesn't feel the environment the character occupies. If an actor doesn't believe in what's happening to the character, why should an audience believe it? If an audience senses that the character in the story they're watching isn't actually where the story says the character is, the show is over.

Human beings constantly measure one another for any signs of dishonesty. An actor who has not established a definitive and absolute sense of the place the character occupies gives all the signs of being a liar. These actors shift their weight uneasily, move stiffly, and exhibit other signs of not belonging where they are. These signs are all clear indications that the actor knows only where the actor is, not where the text says the character is. It's an actor's involuntary body language that isn't part of a character's behavior.

Auditions are particularly challenging to the actor's sense of place. The actor walks into a sterile room, sits down, and tries to engage a casting assistant who reads off of script sides in monotone. There's nothing in the room that the actor can use to *drop in* to a place, on camera and on the first try. The actor has to bring *place* in with him.

Casting agents and directors don't want to see an actor acting any more than an audience does. They want to see life, not work. It's up to you to communicate a character with your body, not with your head. The key to doing that is sensation. When you bring a sensation of place into an audition, you can fill any sterile, cramped space with the life and breath of your character.

WATERLOO

We all have specific places from our pasts that retain personal resonance, year after year. These are places that carry sensation—their smell, their look, the light, and the sound of that locale—decades down the line. Locations where we have experienced moments of disappointment, defeat, tragedy, and unhappiness are the ones that we recall with the strongest emotion and most tactile memory. A **Place of Defeat**—the ball field where a game was lost; the stoop, car, restaurant, or couch where a relationship ended; the hospital bedside where a life ended; a principal's or a boss's office—these locations all have a definitive sensation of place because of the emotional baggage we carry from them.

To explore the parallels between actor and character, I use the Place of Defeat exercise. In the Place of Defeat exercise, you improvise a scenario combining the sensation of a location in which the character suffered disappointment, humiliation, or loss with the sensation of a Place of Defeat from your own past.

For Rosa Parks, your research could send you in any number of directions. Rosa's virtual abandonment by her father, her husband's alcoholism, and her childlessness each suggest locales where Rosa experienced profound defeat, firsthand. The incident I would suggest for Rosa Parks's Place of Defeat took place on another Montgomery, Alabama bus twelve years before Parks's famous 1955 refusal to give up her seat and subsequent arrest.

Since 1896, when the U.S. Supreme Court upheld a Louisiana law that called for separate accommodations for whites on railroads, public transportation and other public facilities in Alabama were kept segregated. When Rosa Parks boarded a Montgomery city bus one afternoon in November, 1943, the Jim Crow laws were in full effect. The ten seats in the front of every Montgomery city bus were reserved for whites only. The ten in the far back were designated for the use of "negroes," as long as a white person didn't want to sit in them. Between these two clearly defined sections were sixteen seats over which the bus driver could exercise his own will. Montgomery City bus drivers were all white men who carried guns and had "police powers" according to bus company policy and Montgomery law.

Some drivers made black riders pay their fare at the front of the bus, and then get off to reenter through the bus's back door. That is, of course, if the driver didn't decide to drive away first, as they often did. On that November day in 1943, the bus that Rosa boarded was crowded with black passengers. She got on the bus at the front, paid her fare, and moved back through the small crowd of white passengers in the front.

The driver, a particularly contemptuous and intimidating man named James Blake, got up and insisted that Rosa exit the bus and reenter through the crowded rear of the bus. She refused, and instead sat down in one of the empty middle seats of the bus. Over Rosa's objections, Blake pulled on Rosa's coat sleeve and dragged her off the bus. It was a scarring humiliation. For the next twelve years, she would scan approaching Cleveland Avenue buses to avoid getting on one driven by the same man.

To establish and explore this Place of Defeat, you would have to learn everything you could about Rosa Parks's life at the time. In addition, you would absorb as much history about American racism in that era, from the persecution of the Scottsboro boys in the '30s to Franklin Roosevelt's desegregation of American military bases in the '40s.

The Place of Defeat exercise would also require the actor playing Rosa to choose a parallel personal incident, so that she has a personal truth with which to anchor the character's reality. I, for instance, have not known discrimination of the vitriolic intensity of Rosa Parks's Alabama; but as an African-American, my life has been touched by bigotry. I am descended from ancestors who were kidnapped from their homeland, bought and sold like mules, whipped, raped, and lynched. Surrendering to this truth would help give me, and any actor doing the place of Defeat exercise as Rosa Parks, a solid parallel truth.

In the early '70s, Harold Clurman offered me the position of understudy for the part of Eve, the lead in a new play called *The Creation of the World and Other Business*. The show was produced by Robert Whitehead, at the time one of the biggest producers on Broadway, and was written by Arthur Miller, author of *Death of a Salesman* and *The Crucible*. By the time the play opened out of town, the other actress had dropped out, and I had the lead. The reviews in Boston were sensational; and when we opened at the Kennedy Center in Washington, D.C., they were just as strong. We were set to open on Broadway after the D.C. run was over. It was the biggest break of my career.

Throughout rehearsals and during the successful trial run in Boston, Robert Whitehead's wife, the actress Zoë Caldwell, had been a fixture backstage. Zoë was a trouper and a Broadway vet of many years. I had never had a lead part like this, and Zoë was very kind to me. She gave me little gifts and advice, and she shared in the triumph of the great notices in Boston and during the previews in D.C.

A few days into the Kennedy Center engagement, Robert Whitehead and Arthur Miller came to see me in my dressing room. "Susan," Whitehead said, "Zoë would like to play the part of Eve. We've decided that she'll be the lead, and that you'll be her understudy. Isn't that wonderful?"

I was shocked. I'd originated the role Miller wrote. Sure, I began as an understudy; but nobody outside of the production knew that, and the reviews were wonderful. Now I was going to be replaced by the producer's wife? Sensations of outrage and anger, loss of dignity, disappointment, and helplessness—I associate those things with that tiny dressing room and the hallway leading to it backstage at the Kennedy Center. Those sensations are as strong now as they were then. That's my Place of Defeat.

You can also apply character Animal Work to the Place of Defeat exercise. Animals naturally have to be attuned to every detail and change in their environment in order to survive. Having humanized the animal's natural heightened physical sensitivity, you should be prepared to see, feel, smell, and hear the sensations of the character's Place of Defeat with an animal's sensitivity. Using Animal helps to transform a neutral environment into a specific and real place.

PLACE OF DEFEAT EXERCISE:

1. The character's Place of Defeat
   e.g. Rosa Parks—a Montgomery, Alabama, bus in 1943

2. The actor's Place of Defeat
   e.g. Backstage at the Kennedy Center

3. The character's humanized animal
   e.g. Rosa Parks—a house cat

Like the Character Private Moment, this exercise is an exploration, *NOT* a performance. The controlling idea of the Place of Defeat exercise is to experience the sensation of a place, not to tell a story. The stage is barren except for any absolutely essential furniture or props. Rosa Parks would only require a chair to represent the seat on the bus.

The actor would have to personalize James Blake, the bus driver. I, for instance, would choose Arthur Miller over Robert Whitehead to use for James Blake. Whitehead was cultured and calm. Jane Alexander once called him "one of the most handsome men I ever saw." But research reveals that James Blake was a large, rough-looking, and intimidating man. Arthur Miller fit that bill. Miller's strongest physical feature was his height. His strongest human quality was an intelligence that had something of a "street" edge to it. Something I will never forget that he said was, "I had no idea you were neurotic," when I dared to object to the demotion he and Whitehead were offering me. There would likely be at least one solid trigger of sensation amongst those Personalization details.

An actor in Rosa Parks's Place of Defeat exercise would gather other personal details of her own Place of Defeat. For instance, the backstage area at the Kennedy Center had grey walls and carpeting. It was very quiet. The dressing room was lit by a makeup mirror, and bare except for a Gauguin print postcard my assistant had put up on the wall. Miller and Whitehead approached me from different directions, like stalking hyenas, and led me into my dressing room before breaking the news. Even though Miller and Whitehead stood in front of and behind me inside the dressing room, I saw them both because of the large makeup mirror on the wall of the very small room.

When James Blake shoved Rosa Parks from his bus, Rosa intentionally dropped her handbag and sat in a white-only seat in the front of the bus to retrieve it. Blake, a tall, heavyset man, stood over tiny Rosa Parks and shouted, "Get off my bus!" Rosa kept her head and warned Blake not to strike her. By this time, even some of the other black passengers were calling out to her to go around to the back so they could be on their way. Rosa was humiliated and furious at the rough treatment from Blake, and ashamed that no one came to her aid or support.

I would center Rosa Parks's Place of Defeat on that moment. An actor improvising this Place of Defeat would use any and all sensations possible from her own Place of Defeat and release them through her imagination. The joy of the exercise is that the actor who becomes Rosa Parks seated on the bus on that November day in 1943 gets to return all the humiliation and say anything she couldn't or didn't say in her own Place of Defeat.

I would search for sensation via the floor of the bus and the grey carpeting that I recall so vividly from the Kennedy Center. I would conjure the same bright light that I recall from the makeup mirrors. James Blake standing over me would have the sensation of imposing, scornful Arthur Miller. The impatient passengers would be a bus full of Robert Whiteheads.

ROSA (seated in chair, screaming): No! No! You cannot do this to me! I am a human being! You have no right to play with my life and with me like this! Why do you do this? Why do the rest of you let him do this? Do you have a sense of God? Of life? *Audemus jura nostra defendere!*

The actor nails the Place of Defeat moment. Her Personalizations were vivid. During her brief outburst the place—the crowded bus interior—flashed to life for a moment as if suddenly lit from darkness. Her touch of using the Alabama State motto, "We dare defend our rights," was particularly inspired. Her anger bore a strong whiff of the cat cornered. She physically recoiled from the sensation of outstretched, aggressive hands. If she can carry this kind of detail and life into an audition, she'll make a lasting impression.

CHAPTER TWENTY

THE CHARACTER INTERVIEW

I want to live every moment totally and intensely.
Even when I'm giving an interview or talking to people,
that's all that I'm thinking about.
Omar Sharif

THE HOT SEAT

Like any other craftsperson, the actor dodges and fields a barrage of decisions, choices, and questions during every working moment. Any truly collaborative creative endeavor tests an artist's commitment, preparation, and ability. Intuition and imagination carry us over many pitfalls in our creative lives; but sometimes we simply have to face inquisitors, and address what they want to know.

Acting can be a daily inquisition. The creation of character opens you up to a bewildering variety of questions. The solid ground of fact and biography that you root a character in can turn to sand if you haven't properly prepared. If you haven't fully worked out the biography, the character will be stillborn. If you don't use your own truth to breathe life into the character, your performance won't live and grow beyond mere fact.

If you are truly "in character," you cannot be shaken by anything: a falling spotlight, a missed line, a sudden ad-lib—nothing that happens to or around you will separate you from your character, if you are prepared. To test the strength of that actor/character union in class, I conduct a Character Interview. By the time of the Character Interview, the actor has engaged in multiple exercises to assist in building the character. The interview tests how effective Animal Work, Character Private Moment, Character Phone Call, and Place of Defeat have been. The Character Interview tests your knowledge of your character and establishes just how completely you have given yourself over to your role.

This exercise itself is essentially a group improvisation. The actor takes a seat, and is questioned by the other actors present. Character interviews take the form of trials, inquisitions, courts-martial, Q&As, press conferences, and debates. The questions asked must challenge the actor's knowledge of the character.

The actor playing Rosa Parks would have to review all of the preparation she's done in creating the character of Rosa so far:

1. The *Public Persona* ("a saint, to care for everyone"), the *Need* ("to be taken care of"), the *Tragic Flaw* ("anger").
2. The Rosa Parks humanized animal—a house cat.

3. The facts of the period—gospel music of the era, newspaper accounts of the Montgomery boycott, as much film footage as she can get her hands on, and so forth.

In addition, she'll have to work out Personalizations for every prominent person from Rosa's life.

A partial list of Personalizations for Rosa Parks:
- Rosa's mother, Leona McCauley
- Rosa's father, James McCauley
- Rosa's husband, Raymond Parks
- Her brother, Sylvester McCauley
- Rosa's friend, E.D. Nixon
- Another mentor, Virginia Durr
- Johnny Mae Carr, childhood friend
- Rosa's teacher, Alice L. White
- The bus driver, James Blake
- Another mentor, Septima Clarke
- Arresting officers, F.B. Day and D.W. Mixon

This character interview would be a routine interrogation of Rosa by her arresting officers on December 1, 1955. Arresting officers, F.B. Day and D.W. Mixon, and some other curious white policemen, will ask her questions while booking her at Montgomery City Hall before taking her to the city jail on North Ripley Street.

TRUTH

ROSA PARKS: CHARACTER INTERVIEW

DAY: It's Rosa P-A-R-K-S?

ROSA: Yes, sir.

DAY: Now, what's your date of birth?

ROSA: February 4, 1913.

DAY: Place of birth?

ROSA: Tuskegee, Alabama.

DAY: Father's name?

ROSA: Why...?

The actor hesitates, dropping in to the sensations she experienced in a Personalization of her own father.

DAY: Father's name?

ROSA: James McCauley. I don't see—

DAY: Mother's name?

ROSA: Oh, my poor mother... Leona Edwards McCauley. She's not well. When can I make a phone call and tell her I'm all right?

Rosa's Public Persona—the caregiver—surfaces.

DAY: I understand you got some family members passing for white.

[Rosa says nothing]

A telling pause. More sensation—the shame and anger from the Character Private Moment.

DAY: I understand your grandfather McCauley was the whitest nigguh that ever lived...

ROSA: Be that as it may, he always kept a double-barreled shotgun close at hand. He was sure that one day he was gonna have the opportunity to blow out one of your kind's brains.

An interesting choice—the actor understands Rosa's passive aggressiveness and the confrontational sense of humor she inherited from her grandfather.

DAY: Married?

ROSA: Yes, and I would like to call my husband.

DAY: Name?

ROSA: My husband's name? Raymond Parks. May I call him?

DAY: Education?

ROSA: High school. I received my diploma in 1933.

DAY: 1933? You got to be the oldest high school graduate in Montgomery.

[They all laugh]

ROSA: It was something my husband encouraged me to do.

A taste of Rosa's Need "to be taken care of."

DAY: Officer Mixon, you got something to ask...um... her?

MIXON: Yeah, I do, FB. Why the hell y'refuse to stand up and give your seat to that white man?

ROSA: Why do you all push us around?

Good research—it's a direct quote from Rosa's autobiography.

MIXON: The law is the law. You know what the law is, don't you?

ROSA: Paying for a seat and riding only a couple blocks and then having to stand was too much...

The Need.

MIXON: Why didn't you stand up?

ROSA [after a silence]: May I please have a drink of—

DAY: No!

ROSA: —water...?

The Need.

ANOTHER OFFICER: No, there ain't a colored water fountain up here. You got any children?

ROSA [tears filling her eyes]: No, I'm childless.

DAY: Your husband a drunk?

TRUTH

Rosa is silent. The actress has gone from the sadness of her unfulfilled Need to the seething rage of her Tragic Flaw.

ANOTHER OFFICER: I understand you been foolin' around with that congressman from New York.

ROSA: Adam Clayton Powell?!

Adam Clayton Powell was a very attractive man.

OFFICER: You got that right. Light-skinned nigguh...

[Rosa glares at him.]

Rosa lapses into the hostile silence of her Tragic Flaw.

OFFICER: Good-looking buck, right?

Rosa, like any seeing person, can't deny Powell's appeal.

ANOTHER OFFICER: You ain't said what the law was that you broke, but you can be sure like we ain't gonna have no Supreme Court changing it like that law last year.

ROSA: *Brown v. Board of Education.* What a great victory. Supreme Court Justice Warren made it clear. That racist Plessey doctrine; separate education is "inherently unequal..."

[Rosa chuckles.]

The actress releases sensation through her laugh.

OFFICER: What's so goddamn funny?

ROSA: You wouldn't understand. Am I just gonna sit here all evening?

OFFICER: Shut up!

ROSA: My feet are swollen, my shoulders are throbbing, I have bursitis. Please do what you have to do with me and let me call my husband?

The Need.

OFFICER ROTH: What does your husband do for a living?

ROSA: He works at the Maxwell Air Force Base barbershop.

ROTH: Do you know the name of the bus driver you refused to obey?

ROSA: Yes, I do. This was my second encounter with this same driver.

ROTH: What's his name?

ROSA: James F. Blake—my first incident with him was in 1943.

Here the actress has slipped. Though Rosa recognized the driver from her earlier run-in twelve years before, she didn't find out his name until her trial, days after her arrest.

DAY: What's the law you broke?

ROSA: It's a cruel and stupid Jim Crow law...

DAY: Answer the question!

ROSA [in tears]: I violated the city's segregation ordinance. There had to be a stopping place, and this seemed to me the place for me to stop being pushed around and to find out what human rights I had, if any...

The Need. The actress has really dropped in.

OFFICER: You ain't nothing but a second-class citizen. Just 'cause you know some white folks don't give you no right to think otherwise.

ROSA: This has gone on long enough. My mother is in frail health, and my husband... Please don't harass him; he has nothing to do with this... Nothing... He is constantly warning me I will be lynched...

OFFICER BART: Mrs. Parks, tell me, as a colored woman, are you ashamed of not having children?

Rosa struggles to keep composure and remain safely within her Public Persona.

ROSA [after a deep breath]: I have many nephews and nieces. They are my brother's children; they live in Detroit. But, I also have many children that I am in contact with through church and the work I do with the NAACP. I come from a very proud people. You have to go a very long way to kill my pride... So, now can this end?

OFFICER: Your father dead or alive?

ROSA: My father is... alive...

Rosa's tears start to flow no matter how hard she tries to hold them back.

I stop the interview. The actor playing Rosa has done a good job. She demonstrated how much of Rosa Parks's biography she has absorbed. Even though she got a few factual details wrong, her strong sensation of Rosa's *Need* and *Public Persona* made up for it. I only wish she had allowed Rosa's *Tragic Flaw* to live more actively. The actor only experiences sensations of *Tragic Flaw*, Rosa's anger, in silences and pauses. She has yet to find a voice for her character's *Tragic Flaw*.

Eastwood De Wayne, the confident, hunky charmer who couldn't loosen up in my circle, has made great strides away from the stiff-legged stud he was on that first day of class. For his Character Interview, Eastwood changes into white slacks and a loud Hawaiian shirt. He takes a seat at a piano and expertly plays a brief Chopin piece that transforms into "I Go to Rio." He has literally become Peter Allen, "The Boy From Oz"; and for the next fifteen minutes, Eastwood answers questions about Allen's early days, his marriage to Liza Minnelli, and his career, in a playful and pitch-perfect Australian accent. It turns out that Eastwood hid more than vulnerability under his Public Persona. Eastwood is himself a great musical talent. He accompanies Peter Allen's breezy answers with brilliant bursts of notes from the piano.

It turns out that musical theater was Eastwood's first love. He's kept his musical ability under wraps since elementary school because he thought it was unmanly. How sad is this world that a talented child would deny his God-given talents in fear of judgment?

SUSAN BATSON

PART

IV

THE SCRIPT

CHAPTER TWENTY-ONE

THE

"CLASSIC C's"

Every moment is a golden one for him
who has vision to reconcile it as such.
Henry Miller

STORY TIME

Human beings are driven, tormented, and redeemed by the same facts, choices, and sensations that drive the characters that populate stories. Those same basic truths of human experience have shaped and defined every story from every era. The love and pain and joy and fear that we feel in ourselves and recognize in each other are what draw us to drama. "The audience doesn't come to see you," Julianne Moore has said. "They come to see themselves." This truth hasn't changed since the dawn of human existence, and it never will. Fundamental, universal humanity is what gives a story relevance and permanence regardless of the language or the society in which the story is set.

The actor's art is the art of creating and interpreting human behavior through a story. In order to do that effectively, the actor has to know the precise dimensions of a story. An actor who doesn't understand the structure and shape of the story his character is in can't hope to effectively communicate through that character. The actor becomes a decoration—a human prop that's no more useful than a portrait painter who doesn't understand perspective and color.

"A story," Jean-Luc Godard once quipped, "should have a beginning, a middle, and an end; but not necessarily in that order." In filmmaking, that's no joke. The practical realities of film production guarantee for the actor that beginning, middle, and end will not line up during shooting. Location, cast availability, and other production requirements shatter linear story chronology during principal photography. That chronology is then restored and honed in the editing room long after the actor is onto his next job. For the sake of production, an actor may have to shoot his character's death scene on one day, and his wedding night the next.

If you don't have a rock-solid grasp on the arc of the script, you'll lose the story's truth in the shooting schedule's necessary chaos. You have to know your script so well that the truth of your character survives the production process intact.

FROM CIRCUMSTANCES TO CONCLUSION

A story, no matter what the genre or style, begins with "The Five C's":

1. Circumstances
2. Conflict
3. Crisis
4. Climax
5. Conclusion

Whether in a traditional narrative like *Gone With the Wind* or *Death of a Salesman*; a broad-canvas, multi-plotted film like *Magnolia, Crash,* or *Nashville*; a seemingly plotless pseudo documentary like *Keane*; or a musical like *Dream Girls*, the five Cs are there. They're clear markers of a character's dramatic life and a story's progression. An actor who wishes to do truthful work must use these markers to correctly position a character at any given point in the story.

CIRCUMSTANCES

Circumstances (or "given circumstances") are facts. What are the facts of the story's world?

It's early in World War II.

Morocco has become an embarkation point for refugees fleeing Nazi persecution.

An expatriate American runs a nightclub there.

The American receives stolen documents for safekeeping.

The great lost love of his life arrives in Morocco.

Her new husband is a freedom fighter desperately wanted by the Gestapo.

She has to have the documents in order to escape from the Nazis with her husband.

The American and his lost love are still very much in love with one another.

—*Casablanca*

A Memphis pimp is closing in on fatherhood, and wants more out of life than he has.

He assembles a few collaborators to make a hip-hop record.

He has to use his street smarts to get his record made and heard.

—*Hustle and Flow*

After he is visited by a deranged ex-patient, a Philadelphia child psychiatrist struggles to understand how the experience has changed him.

He begins to work with a disturbed young boy who believes he can see the spirits of the dead walking amongst us.

The boy actually does have that gift.

The psychiatrist discovers that he is himself dead—a victim of the fateful encounter with his ex-patient.

—*The Sixth Sense*

These story circumstances are not a matter of opinion or of belief; they are simple, given facts. No matter how heady or emotional a story gets, a fact is always a fact. These facts—the story's circumstances—are the actor's anchor.

SUSAN BATSON

CONFLICT

Conflict is the energy that moves a story forward. Without conflict, there is nothing to be done, no questions to be asked, no risk, no growth, and no change. Your actor must sniff out conflict like a bloodhound. You must embrace it, and make it as true for you as it is for your character. Conflict is the lifeblood of drama— "the music of story," as Robert McKee says.

It takes two forces to provoke conflict. On one side is the protagonist force. The Protagonist moves forward through the story. Without opposition, there is no conflict. The antagonist is that opposition. An antagonist character or force blocks the protagonist's forward movement.

For the contemporary actor, the variation in story styles and writers' intentions sometimes make the specific protagonist/ antagonist conflict difficult to see. In any scene, the protagonist is any character or element that moves the story action forward. The antagonist is any character or element of conflict that blocks that forward movement. Wherever there is conflict, there is a protagonist force attempting to move forward, and an antagonist force attempting to block its progress.

The actor must understand what his character's relationship is to the protagonist/antagonist conflict. Even if you only have a minor role, a single line, or a reaction shot, you must know which team you're on. An actor who doesn't know which side of the protagonist/antagonist fence he occupies cannot tell the story.

Is your character on the antagonist side with the racist status quo in *Crash*, or the protagonist side with individuals trying to live their lives beyond the stereotypes that the antagonist force perpetuates? Are you on the protagonist side with love, family, and responsibility in *Magnolia*, or on the antagonist side with self-involvement and emotional exile?

Whether protagonist or antagonist, conflict comes in two strains. *Internal conflicts* are struggles within the character about the character's own nature. Internal conflicts often involve issues of self-knowledge and identity (e.g. "Who am I?") in films such as *Fight Club* and *The Bourne Identity*.

Circumstantial conflicts involve the facts of interpersonal issues (e.g. unrequited love), as in *Bringing up Baby* and *Eternal Sunshine of the Spotless Mind*; or physical risks or threats, as in heroic journeys like *Deep Impact* and *The Last Samurai*.

Most characters struggle with both levels of conflict. Throughout *Requiem for a Dream*, Harry Goldfarb deals with internal conflict—his self-destructive desire for escape into drug-induced oblivion—while he shoulders circumstantial conflicts between himself and his mother from whom he steals, his girlfriend whom he's unable to protect, the gangsters who have enslaved him, and the cops that would put him away.

Circumstances force a protagonist into conflict. As the story progresses, and the protagonist's actions succeed or fail, the conflict deepens and intensifies. The protagonist pushes, and the antagonist pushes back, until the protagonist and antagonist reach the point of crisis.

POINT OF CRISIS

By the time a story arrives at its point of crisis, there is no turning back. Sam, Annie, and Jonah are all on their way to the Empire State Building in *Sleepless in Seattle*. Rick Blaine takes the letters of transit to the airfield to rendezvous with Ilsa in *Casablanca*. "Now I see this clearly," says *Taxi Driver's* Travis Bickle as he readies himself to assassinate a U.S. senator. "My whole life is pointed in one direction. There never has been a choice for me." But Travis, like all Protagonists, does have a choice; and in crisis, he is pushed to make the most important choice of the story.

CLIMAX

In the climax, we find out what the protagonist's choice is. Travis kills a pimp and other criminal lowlifes, not a political candidate. Sam decides to wait with Jonah at the top of the Empire State Building, leaves, returns for Jonah's knapsack, and finds Annie. Rick Blaine shoots a Gestapo major and puts Ilsa and her husband on a plane to freedom.

Climax is the ultimate expression of conflict and crisis. It's the moment in which the actions that a protagonist has taken to fulfill his *Need* ultimately do or don't pay off.

CONCLUSION

Finally, in the denouement, we see the results of the climax. The conclusion communicates what has changed for the protagonist and his world. It's where we learn what the character has lost or gained as he has worked through to the climax of the story. *The Godfather's* Michael Corleone comforts the sister whose husband he ordered murdered. He then closes the door on his own wife and any hope of a normal family life outside of the Mafia. Rick and Louis set off to join the French Resistance in *Casablanca*.

In *Traffic*, there are three conclusions. Mexican policeman Javier Rodriguez watches a ball game in the new baseball diamond that was the price he put on cooperation with the American DEA. Rodriguez has at last done something that is clearly for the greater good of the community he serves. American cop Montel Gordon reveals that his seemingly pointless confrontation with Helena Ayala was a ruse for placing a listening device in her home, with which he will keep tabs on her. Robert Wakefield attends his daughter Caroline's Narcotics Anonymous meeting. He honestly connects with Caroline in a way that was never before possible.

A story starts with characters and the facts of their world. It moves forward on conflict. It climbs through a crisis, peaks at a climax when everything they've been holding back comes out, and comes back down to a conclusion where what's just come to pass changes those people and their world.

Think of it as being like sex: Circumstances bring you together. Conflict has you engage each other—flirting, making out. Point of crisis is when you're getting down to it; and climax is—well, do I have to spell it out? The conclusion suggests what's different afterwards. A cigarette? Deep sleep in each other's arms? A feast? A separation? One more time? All climaxes have different aftermaths.

OTHELLO

By

William Shakespeare

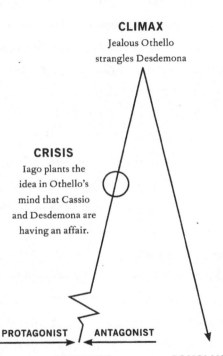

CLIMAX
Jealous Othello
strangles Desdemona

CRISIS
Iago plants the
idea in Othello's
mind that Cassio
and Desdemona are
having an affair.

PROTAGONIST ANTAGONIST

CIRCUMSTANCES
Othello the Moor has
eloped with Desdemona.
Iago, Othello's lieutenant
has turned against Othello
and plots to destroy him.

CONFLICT
Protagonist Othello
heads toward the truth.
Antagonist Iago
heaps lie upon lie

CONCLUSION
Othello and Desdemona
are together forever.
"I kiss thee ere I kill'd
thee. No way but this,
killing myself, to die
upon a kiss."

CIRCUMSTANCES

As William Shakespeare's *Othello* begins, Othello the Moor, a mighty North African warrior in the service of the king of Venice, has eloped with Desdemona, the beautiful white daughter of Brabantio, a powerful and racist Venetian senator. One of Othello's lieutenants, a trusted advisor named Iago, has secretly turned against Othello after losing a promotion to the more virtuous Cassio. Together, Iago and Rodrigo, Desdemona's spurned suitor, plot to destroy Othello. Iago dispatches Rodrigo to inform the senator of his daughter's forbidden marriage in the most inflammatory words possible.

CONFLICT

The conflict between antagonist Iago and protagonist Othello is a matter of deception and manipulation. Protagonist Othello wrongly assumes that Iago is trustworthy. Othello leads the protagonist team. He heads toward the truth.

Antagonist Iago is driven by jealousy and by a desire to subordinate and enslave the Moor. Iago believes that once he has destroyed Othello, he will possess his soul. Iago leads the antagonist team, heaping lie upon lie to obstruct, topple, and enslave Othello.

CRISIS

The point of crisis arrives when Iago plants a handkerchief that Othello has given Desdemona on Cassio. Iago suggests to Othello that Cassio and Desdemona are having an affair. Othello's suspicion of Desdemona moves closer to confront-ation. Iago pushes him further by manipulating a conversation that Othello overhears and believes to be Cassio and Desdemona (who it isn't).

CLIMAX

The play climaxes as Othello strangles Desdemona. She dies "a guiltless death."

CONCLUSION

In the conclusion, Cassio and Iago's wife Emelia reveal all that Iago has done to Othello. Othello stabs and wounds Iago, then turns a dagger on himself. Mortally wounded, Othello falls next to the lifeless Desdemona. "I kiss thee ere I kill'd thee. No way but this, killing myself, to die upon a kiss."

BROKEBACK MOUNTAIN

By

E. Annie Proulx, Larry McMurtry, and Diana Ossana

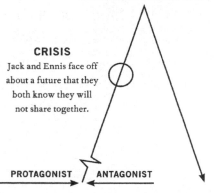

CLIMAX

Jack's wife tells Ennis that Jack was killed in an accident. Ennis sees the truth.

CRISIS

Jack and Ennis face off about a future that they both know they will not share together.

PROTAGONIST   ANTAGONIST

CIRCUMSTANCES

Ennis and Jack work together in the remote Wyoming wilderness. Jack makes the first move and the two men become lovers.

CONFLICT

Jack and Ennis are a two-man protagonist force facing the combined antagonism of nature, an intolerant society, everyone from whom they hide their love, and their own individual internal conflicts involving Jack's desire for other men and Ennis' inability to commit to Jack or to anyone else.

CONCLUSION

One cowboy, two shirts. "Jack, I swear..."

CIRCUMSTANCES

In the early 1960s, Ennis, a taciturn young ranch hand, and Jack, a brash young rodeo cowboy work together as sheepherders in the remote Wyoming wilderness. Jack has had homosexual experiences in the past. The hardships the two men endure together bring them closer and closer together until one night they get drunk and wind up sharing a tent under the full moon. Jack makes the first move, but Ennis takes control. Ennis says it's "a one-shot thing," but the two men have become lovers.

CONFLICT

Brokeback Mountain has multiple conflicts that fan out over the story's two decades. Jack and Ennis form a two-man protagonist force initially in circumstantial conflict with the antagonist force of nature—a marauding bear, the harsh weather, the full moon. As the story goes on, their dual protagonist force faces the circumstantial antagonist force of an intolerant society, their wives, and everyone else from whom they hide their love.

As the decades go on, Jack wrestles with an internal conflict that pits the positive force of his real love for Ennis against his reckless desire to find pleasure with other men. Ennis struggles with an internal conflict that keeps him from fully committing to Jack or anyone else in his life. "If you can't fix it," he tells Jack, "you gotta stand it."

CRISIS

Ennis lets his family responsibilities get in the way of periodic rendezvous with Jack. Ennis's wife divorces him. Jack takes up with another man. Ennis passively lets a relationship with another woman that loves him slip through his fingers. On one of their liaisons, Jack and Ennis, now entering their forties, face off about a future they both know they will not share together. "There's never enough time," Jack says. Pressed by Jack, Ennis reveals the toll his inability to commit has cost him. "I'm nothing, I'm nowhere," he says. They separate once again.

CLIMAX

Months after their last meeting, Ennis's postcard to Jack suggesting a rendezvous gets returned marked "Deceased." He calls Jack's wife. She tells him her husband was killed in an accident. Ennis knows Jack was killed by a homophobic lynch mob.

CONCLUSION

At Jack's parents' house, Ennis finds a shirt of his and a shirt of Jack's that Jack had secretly hung together. Ennis takes the shirts and enshrines them in his trailer alongside a picture of Brokeback Mountain, a place he will never leave, yet never return to. Acknowledging his commitment at last, he blesses the shirts with the words, "Jack, I swear...."

CHAPTER TWENTY-TWO

THE SCRIPT BREAKDOWN

Words may show a man's wit, but actions his meaning.

Benjamin Franklin

If it were all in the script, why make the film?

Nicholas Ray

"HOW DID YOU LEARN ALL THOSE LINES?"

Acting holds many mysteries to the civilian. From the outside looking in, committing an entire Play's worth of dialogue to memory appears to be a Herculean task. The civilian assumes that the actor's job is to memorize an entire script, along with a grocery list of gestures, movements, and emotional deliveries.

The actor is responsible for telling the story through human behavior. Your relationship with the text—the dialogue and stage directions indicated in the description—is actually very simple. You must fully embrace the writer's words. You don't learn the text. The text *goes in* to you. Memorization won't make that happen. You *get the text in* by making a connection to the writer. You immerse yourself in the emotional, psychological, and physical energy of the writer's words—the text's action.

From my earliest days in children's theater, I understood that learning dialogue wasn't about memorizing the words on the page as much as it was about letting the writer's words into my psyche. I would sleep with the script under my pillow, carry it with me everywhere, write and rewrite the words in a notebook—anything that would allow the words to find a way into me and guide my imagination.

But when I took over the lead in *The Creation of the World and Other Business*, I had to learn the entire script in a matter of days. We were opening in Boston at the end of the week, and I was petrified. There wasn't time for me to use any of my old tricks. But the show's director, Harold Clurman, a Group Theatre veteran and truly one of the great directors, critics, and teachers of all time, took pity on me. To my surprise he said, "I'm going to teach you to not memorize."

What Clurman taught me was how to break down the script in a way that made the playwright's words so clear, and my responsibility to the character so specific, that there wasn't any reason to memorize. Using Harold Clurman's system, I learned the actions behind the text, not the lines themselves. Knowing the actions makes the text an organic part of the character's experience, not a litany of lifeless statements and questions that the actor parrots verbatim.

Through Script Breakdown, I examined each word with the same intensity, and from the same variety of levels, with which I looked at character. Methodically breaking a text down into actions enables the actor to absorb the full meaning of the writer's words. Clurman's system allowed me to establish and maintain a unique, unshakably strong relationship with the text. Even if the play was written four-hundred years before I was born, the Script Breakdown brought the writer and me into closer collaboration than I ever knew was possible.

The actor who masters this system will own the text. Your memory will take its cues from the preparatory work you've done. You'll connect with the script using your own emotional and sensory experience. When that breakdown is thorough, detailed, and complete, the actor learns the script without memorizing. Know the action and the line will come.

Script Breakdown also provides an understanding of the continuity of the story that even the cruelest constant reshuffling of scenes won't dislodge. If you do the work, then you'll know the lines. If you apply yourself to the breakdown, you'll always know where you are in the story's arc. You won't have to play the good student cramming for a final. Instead, you'll be an artist using your skill and imagination to collaborate and to create by "taking something that's nothing more than ink, and transforming it into behavior," as Robert Duvall put it in an interview.

BEAT BY BEAT

The fundamental building block of a script is the beat. Each beat is a single complete dramatic thought—a moment. A beat is whole when it completes a dramatic thought, not just initiates one. Identifying a beat requires that you read down the text until a dramatic thought feels like a complete moment. The next beat is the following moment, and so on. Each beat picks up from the end of the previous complete dramatic thought.

No matter how quiet or tacit their *Public Personas* may be, all characters are constantly in action working to fulfill their Needs. Hattie in *Sweet and Lowdown* and Chief Bromden in *One Flew Over the Cuckoo's Nest* are nearly completely silent for the course of both films. Yet they are both tremendously active characters who are doggedly working to fulfill their respective *Needs*. Hattie *Needs* "to be loved" and Chief Bromden *Needs* "to be free." They communicate those *Needs* to the audience by the choices they make—through their *actions*.

No one just says words. There is always an action behind the words that a character speaks. No one just hears words either. Listening, hearing, and reacting to another character's words always have an action behind them. Characters don't turn themselves on and off like robots when another character is speaking or moving. Only bad actors do that.

The vehicle the actor uses to send the writer's words to the audience is action. No matter who is talking, every character has an action for every beat. And for every one of these actions there is a transitive verb that describes it—"to accuse," "to beg," "to toy," "to ignore," "to make peace," "to belittle," "to praise," "to seduce," "to condemn," "to reassure."

Characters don't fulfill their *Needs*, work their *Public Personas*, or jam up in their *Tragic Flaws* through unwieldy intellectualizations. No matter how arch or heady the dialogue, there are simple, direct actions that the actor uses to engage the other characters. The simpler and more active the verb describing an action, the stronger the drama.

There are five categories that can be used to describe any beat. They are the five *writer's tools*:

1. Exposition
2. Character Statement
3. Statement of Need
4. Statement of Conflict
5. Operative

When breaking down the text, the actor assigns one of these five writer's tools to every single beat in the script. Each beat has a corresponding tool—Exposition, Operative, Statement of Conflict, and so on. The tool designated for each beat is the same for each character in the scene. These tools never repeat back to back. There are never two Statements of Conflict or two Operative beats in a row. If two beats in a row seem to call for the same category, there's something wrong with the text or the actor's understanding of the text.

EXPOSITION

Exposition is fact. Straight up, pure and simple—"Luke, I'm your father," "Iceberg, dead ahead!" "I am not a Communist," "Houston, we have a problem"—an exposition beat is a statement of fact. An Exposition beat always has the same action: "to tell the truth."

In an effort to attach all the energy and meaning they can to every word in the text, many actors forget that the action in an

Exposition beat is simply "to tell the truth." Playing Eve in *The Creation of the World and Other Business*, the script called for me to say, "This is my son Cain, and this is my son Abel," alongside the two actors playing Cain and Abel. Both actors were white. One was older than me, the other (a blond) was my age exactly.

I decided that the only way I could make the line true was to make it about how hurt and disappointed Eve was with her sons, and their animosity toward one another. When I said Cain's name, I figured I would speak through this painful disappointment I had personalized. I went to rehearsal, we did the scene, and when I got to that line, I said it with all the tears and the anguish I had in me.

Clurman exploded! "What did I tell you to do in an Exposition beat?" he demanded. "State the facts, state the facts, state the facts!" In every performance after that, I followed his instruction. I stood there and just said, "This is my son Cain, and this is my son Abel," as the plain, simple truth that it was in the text. And every night without fail, the audience would sigh an approving "oh-h-h-h" in perfect unison. No laughter, no shrugs, no perplexed looks—every night they bought it, hook, line, and sinker.

If I did not state the line as the fact that it was; if I didn't make sure that the fact was clear, the audience would've looked at me, looked at the two guys playing my sons, and been completely confused. By stating the facts, I told the story.

CHARACTER STATEMENT

A Character Statement works like an adjective. The playwright uses the Character Statement to describe a person, a place, or a thing. Film scripts tend to contain fewer Character Statements than plays, because film is inherently more visual. The Character Statement doesn't expose; it describes. You use actions of personality for a Character Statement. "To charm," "to flatter," "to toy," "to showboat," "to dance around an issue," "to joke," "to rhapsodize"—these are the kinds of action choices that send the meaning of a Character Statement.

STATEMENT OF NEED

These beats are tied up in the internal, emotional, psychological life of the character. Need beats can directly address the unfulfilled *Need* that a character's *Public Persona* covers, or another psychological or emotional need at work in a scene. The action accompanying a *Need* beat is always "to reveal" or "to expose" an emotional state, a desire, a want, a wish, or an obsession. "To reveal a weakness," "to expose a wound," "to confess a feeling"; these are the kinds of verb choices Statements of *Need* suggest.

When a writer uses a pause, it's another Statement of *Need*. In a pause, actors drop in to their character's *Need*, and then come out of it into the next moment. Pauses are mini-Character Private Moments.

STATEMENTS OF CONFLICT

Statements of Conflict, like conflict itself, are either internal—within the character—or circumstantial—between characters or other outside forces. Statements of Conflict require competitive, confrontational verbs for their actions—"to fight," "to block," "to force," "to needle," "to attack," "to crush," "to demand," "to accuse"—actions that carry an aggressive, combative energy.

OPERATIVE

Operative beats are beats that move the story forward. Entrances, exits, answering ringing phones, asking questions—any beat that urges the story itself along is an Operative beat. Operative beat actions are often directly spelled out in the language of a character parenthetical, stage direction, or description in the text. When an Operative beat is spelled out in the text itself, the action is simply "to do as given"—just do as the text says. Otherwise the action of an Operative beat is a strong, transitive action verb, like "to push," "to provoke," "to seduce," "to run away from," or "to pressure."

CHAPTER TWENTY-THREE

THE SIDES

*Words mean more than what is set down on paper. It takes the
human voice to infuse them with shades of deeper meaning.*
Maya Angelou

LOOK CLOSER

This scene is on page ninety-one of the published version of
Alan Ball's Oscar-winning script for *American Beauty*. It's a short
but key scene just prior to the climax of the story. I'll identify and
mark the beats in the scene and go through them for either
character the same way that I would if I were working with actors
who were playing the parts.

As we go through the scene, we'll pencil in a slash mark on
the script at the end of each beat. Each beat also gets numbered at
the slash mark.

INT. BURNHAM HOUSE — FAMILY ROOM — CONTINUOUS

HIS POV: AS we MOVE SLOWLY around a corner, Angela comes
into view, standing at the STEREO, holding a CD case. She's
been crying; her face is puffy, and her hair mussed. She
regards us apprehensively... then puts on a slightly
defiant smile.

> ANGELA
> I hope you don't mind if I play
> the stereo.

Lester leans against the wall and takes a swig of his beer.

> LESTER
1--- Not at all.
> (then)
2--- Bad night?

> ANGELA
> Not really bad, just... strange.

> LESTER
> (grins)
> Believe me. It couldn't possibly
> be any stranger than mine.

She smiles. ---3
They stand there in silence; the atmosphere is charged.

> ANGELA
> Jane and I had a fight.
> (after a beat)
> It was about you.

She's trying to be seductive as she says this, but she's
pretty bad at it. Lester raises his eyebrows.

> ANGELA (CONT'D)
4--- She's mad at me because I said I
> think you're sexy.

Lester grins. He is sexy.

> LESTER
> (offering a beer)
> Do you want a sip?

SUSAN BATSON

She nods. Lester holds the bottle up to her mouth and she
drinks clumsily. He gently wipes her chin with the back of
his hand.

>   LESTER (CONT'D)
>   So... are you going to tell me
>   what you want?

>   ANGELA
>   I don't know.

>   LESTER

5 - - - You don't know?

His face is very close to hers. She's unnerved--this is
happening too fast...

>   ANGELA
>   What do you want?

>   LESTER
>   Are you kidding? I want you. I've
>   wanted you since the first moment
>   I saw you. You are the most
>   beautiful thing I have ever seen.

Angela takes a deep breath just before Lester leans in to
kiss her cheeks, her forehead, her eyelids, her neck...

>   ANGELA
>   You don't think I'm ordinary?

>   LESTER
>   You couldn't be ordinary if you
>   tried.

>   ANGELA
> 6 - - -   Thank you.
>   (far away)
>   I don't think there's anything
> 7 - - - worse than being ordinary...

And Lester kisses her on the lips...   - - - 8

TRUTH

We'll use the chart below to list and organize the beats by number. As we go through the scene beat by beat, write the number of each successive beat in that "Beat" column. Numbering the beats keeps them straight for the actor. It's also efficient for me when I'm working with an actor on set. If there's a difference in interpretation, some confusion or difficulty, I can specifically deal with each numbered beat and keep them all straight even on the phone.

The second column is where the actor identifies which of the playwright's five tools each beat is. The third column is labeled "Action." In this column, write the rock-solid transitive verb or verb phrase that best describes what the character's action is in that beat.

Just breaking the script down and identifying and numbering its component parts would be pointless. The Script Breakdown isn't complete unless the actor uses it to contribute his own truth to the writer's words. The fourth column is labeled "Personalized Material." This is where you list your own sensations, Personalizations, and Sense Memory triggers, appropriate to each beat.

Script Breakdown

Title: Character:

Beat:	Description:	Action:	Personalized Material

ANGELA'S SIDE

In the previous scene, Angela Hayes, a teenage girl, whose *Need* "to be adored" at a pure, innocent level lies beneath a common cynical teenage seductress *Public Persona*, has just had a nasty argument with Lester Burnham's daughter Jane and Jane's boyfriend Ricky. Lester is plainly attracted to Angela; and, to Jane's disgust, Angela is doing nothing to slow his advances. Jane's words are sharp and accurate. They cut through Angela's *Public Persona*.

As the scene begins, Lester finds Angela playing music and trying to get her shattered manipulative nymphet act going again. The first beat, the scene's first complete dramatic thought, ends as Lester swigs his beer and tells Angela, "Not at all."

```
INT. BURNHAM HOUSE — FAMILY ROOM — CONTINUOUS

His POV: As we MOVE SLOWLY around a corner, Angela
comes into view, standing at the STEREO, holding a CD
case. She's been crying; her face is puffy, and her
hair mussed. She regards us apprehensively... then
puts on a slightly defiant smile.

                    ANGELA
          I hope you don't mind if I play the
          stereo.

Lester leans against the wall and takes a swig of his
beer.

                    LESTER
      I--- Not at all.
```

This is a Statement of Character for Angela. The action behind the beat for her is "to play the good girl."

The number of the beat, and the last word or two of the beat itself, go into column one. "Character" goes into column two; and "to play the innocent" goes into column three. Column four gets the personal material—a Personalization, a Sense Memory, an experience, or a place that gives the actor the sensation of the action "to play the good girl." A Personalization of an attractive older man or a similar crush object would be good territory for an actor playing Angela to explore.

Script Breakdown

Title: *American Beauty*   **Character:** *Angela*

Beat:	Description:	Action:	Personalized Material
1. " ...at all."	*Character Statement*	*To play good girl for him*	

Lester asks Angela, "Bad night?" That's a moment in itself, a complete dramatic thought that becomes the second beat. It gives Angela an opening, it ramps up the narrative, and it moves the story forward. This second beat is Operative.

Angela is paying close attention to Lester, letting him engage her. The action, then, would be "to be pulled in to his warmth/concern." The actor's personalized material would have to embody the same kind of accommodating warmth.

```
                        LESTER
    |---   Not at all.
                   (then)
    2---   Bad night?


                        ANGELA
          Not really bad, just... strange.


                        LESTER
                   (grins)
          Believe me. It couldn't possibly
          be any stranger than mine.

    She smiles.  ---3
    They stand there in silence; the atmosphere is charged.
```

The third beat ends with Angela's smile. This is another Character Statement. She *has* had a bad night, but chooses to downgrade it to "strange" for Lester's benefit. She's telling him what she thinks will make her appear appealing to him, what she believes he wants to hear. She's being attentive to what he's saying, despite having no idea what he's actually talking about. The action behind Angela's smile is "to sweet-talk him." The personalized material could be another Personalization, perhaps the same as in the first beat.

Beat:	Description:	Action:	Personalized Material
2. " bad night?"	Operative	To be pulled into his warmth/concern	
3. " she smiles"	Character Statement	To sweet-talk him	

Angela next describes the argument she's just had with Lester's daughter Jane. This fourth beat ends with "I said I think you're sexy." Angela *did* say it. Jane really *is* mad at her. It's a fact—an Exposition beat—and, as with all Exposition beats, her action is "to tell the truth." Personalized material would come from a time or place or person that carries a *Need* "to tell the truth" in the actor's life.

>   ANGELA
>   Jane and I had a fight.
>   (after a beat)
>   It was about you.
>
> She's trying to be seductive as she says this, but she's
> pretty bad at it. Lester raises his eyebrows.
>
>   ANGELA (CONT'D)
>   She's mad at me because I said I
>   think you're sexy. ---4

Beat:	Description:	Action:	Personalized Material
4. "you're sexy"	Exposition	To tell the truth	

The next complete dramatic thought covers Lester giving Angela a sip of his beer, wiping her chin seductively, asking her what she wants, and leaning in close to her. The moment ends with Angela asking Lester, "What do you want?"

The question moves the scene and the story forward. The fifth beat is another Operative beat. What they've been talking around is now coming to the fore. This Operative beat takes the scene to the next dramatic level. It's happening more quickly than Angela would like. The accompanying action, "to question him," is simple, clear, and active.

```
                    LESTER
               (offering a beer)
          Do you want a sip?
```

She nods. Lester holds the bottle up to her mouth and she drinks clumsily. He gently wipes her chin with the back of his hand.

```
                 LESTER (CONT'D)
          So... are you going to tell me?
          What you want?
```

```
                    ANGELA
          I don't know.
```

```
                    LESTER
          You don't know?
```

His face is very close to hers. She's unnerved--this is happening too fast...

```
                    ANGELA
          What do you want? ---5
```

Beat:	Description:	Action:	Personalized Material
5. "You want?	Operative	To question him	

The next beat ends with Angela saying, "Thank you." Still stinging from Ricky condemning her as "ordinary," she desperately wants to hear what Lester's saying—so desperately that she'll ignore her growing discomfort. Beat number six is a *Need* beat. She's revealing her *Need* "to be adored."

```
                    LESTER
          Are you kidding? I've wanted you
          since the first moment I saw you.
          You are most beautiful thing I
          have ever seen.
```

SUSAN BATSON

```
Angela takes a deep breath just before Lester leans in to
kiss her cheek, her forehead, her eyelids, her neck...

                    ANGELA
          You don't think I'm ordinary?

                    LESTER
          You couldn't be ordinary if you
          tried.

                    ANGELA
          Thank you. ---6
              (far away)
          I don't think there's anything
          worse than being ordinary...---7
```

"I don't think there's anything worse than being ordinary" is the seventh beat. It's a Conflict beat, a moment that reveals a lot about Angela, her *Need*, *Public Persona*, and *Tragic Flaw*. Angela's inner conflict is between her innocent *Need* "to be adored" and her flirty sex kitten *Public Persona*. Angela wants to be special, but settles for any kind of attention. Angela's *Tragic Flaw* is operating—she's lowering herself, giving herself away. She does feel ordinary, and she'll do anything to rid herself of that feeling. Her circumstantial conflict is with Lester; she's the antagonist to his protagonist. Her action is "to hide her ordinariness."

```
And Lester kisses her on the lips.  ---8
```

As the scene ends, Lester kisses her on the lips. Unlike Lester's kisses to her cheek, this kiss is a complete dramatic thought in itself. Beat number eight is as Operative as a beat gets. The scene ends on it. Heavy complications open up for both characters. Even though Angela's yielding, she's trading her body for the adoration she needs. It's a solid, active beat for her: "to take what she wants from him."

Beat:	Description:	Action:	Personalized Material
6. "thank you"	Need	To reveal her Need to be adored	
7. "...being ordinary"	Conflict	To hide her ordinariness	
8. "on the lips"	Operative	To take what she wants from him	

Lester's Side

At various times throughout *American Beauty*, there are sequences that meticulously depict Lester Burnham's fantasies and dreams. He fantasizes about being with a teenage girl, but what we see isn't images of sweating backs and coupling bodies. Lester fantasizes about Angela amidst rose petals and soft light. That's where Lester's *Need* is spelled out. Lester's *Need* is "to know beauty." His protagonist force is the search for that beauty. Lester's *Public Persona* is a suburban everyman. He's the bitter head of a dysfunctional household and is in the throes of a youth-obsessed midlife crisis.

When Lester's *Need* for purity jams up against his off-the-rack Mr. Suburbia *Public Persona*, he is powerless. He tosses off his job, he's unable to seduce his own wife, he's incapable of uniting or inspiring his family, and he won't shoulder any responsibility, control his hedonistic appetite, or mollify his violent, closeted neighbor. That powerlessness is Lester's *Tragic Flaw*.

In the moments before the first beat of the scene, Lester has rebuffed Ricky's father's advances. As the scene begins, Lester reassures Angela that it is okay to be where she is and doing what she's doing. In that first beat, Lester makes a Statement of Character. He's sloughing off responsibility and choosing "to play Mr. Cool." The actor's personal material would be to personalize someone who is a sexual turn-on.

Asking Angela about her bad night in beat number two, an Operative beat, moves the story forward. His action is "to feign concern." Beat three, Lester's admission of how strange his own night has been, ends with Angela's smile. In this Statement of Character he's trying "to be one of the kids."

INT. BURNHAM HOUSE — FAMILY ROOM — CONTINUOUS

HIS POV: AS we MOVE SLOWLY around a corner, Angela comes into view, standing at the STEREO, holding a CD case. She's been crying; her face is puffy, and her hair mussed. She regards us apprehensively... then puts on a slightly defiant smile.

                    ANGELA
          I hope you don't mind if I play
          the stereo.

Lester leans against the wall and takes a swig of his beer.
                    LESTER
   1---   Not at all.
               (then)
   2---   Bad night?
                    ANGELA
          Not really bad, just... strange.
                    LESTER
               (grins)
          Believe me. It couldn't possibly
          be any stranger than mine.

She smiles. ---3
They stand there in silence; the atmosphere is charged.

TRUTH

> ANGELA
> Jane and I had a fight.
> (after a beat)
> It was about you.

She's trying to be seductive as she says this, but she's pretty bad at it. Lester raises his eyebrows.

> ANGELA (CONT'D)
> 4--- She's mad at me because I said I
> think you're sexy.

Script Breakdown

Title: *American Beauty*   **Character:** *Angela*

Beat:	Description:	Action:	Personalized Material
1. "...at all."	Character Statement	To play "Mr. Cool"	
2. "bad night?"	Operative	To feign concern	
3. "she smiles."	Character Statement	To be one of the kids	
4. "you're sexy."	Exposition	To receive that fact	

Lester is on the receiving end of beat four's Exposition. Since Lester is listening to something true, not saying it, his action is "to receive the facts." In beat five Lester has tipped his hand and the story is moving forward. His action in this Operative beat is "to seduce." The actor may want to explore an overall sensation of horniness and desire. The following beat, ending with Angela's "Thank you," is a Need beat for Lester. His desire for her is out in the open; his action in beat six is "to expose his hunger."

ANGELA
I don't know.

LESTER

5 --- You don't know?

His face is very close to hers. She's unnerved--this is
happening too fast...

ANGELA
What do you want?

LESTER
Are you kidding? I want you. I've
wanted you since the first moment
I saw you. You are the most
beautiful thing I have ever seen.

Angela takes a deep breath just before Lester leans in to
kiss her cheeks, her forehead, her eyelids, her neck...

ANGELA
You don't think I'm ordinary?

LESTER
You couldn't be ordinary if you
tried.

ANGELA

6 --- Thank you.

Beat:	Description:	Action:	Personalized Material
5. "...you want?"	Operative	To seduce	
6. "thank you."	Need	To expose his hunger	

The next beat is tricky. Since Lester's *Need* is "to know
beauty" and seek love with romantic purity, giving in to Angela's
manufactured, fraudulent sensuality represents a Statement of

TRUTH

Conflict. Lester recognizes on some level that what he's about to have with Angela will evoke the soft light and rose-petal perfection of his fantasies. But the perfection that Lester seeks doesn't mean a furtive tryst with a frightened teenage girl whose feelings have just been gravely hurt. He should be worshipping her; but instead, in *Tragic Flaw*, Lester's powerless in the face of his carnal desire. Lester's protagonist force is blocked. By surrendering to him, Angela embodies the antagonist force of the scene. It's an inner conflict for Lester. His action is "to take her."

                              ANGELA
    6 — — —   Thank you.
                         (far away)
                   I don't think there's anything
    7 — — — worse than being ordinary...

    And Lester kisses her on the lips.. — — — 8

Finally, their kiss in beat eight is Operative for Lester, just as it was for Angela. They're moving the story along to the climax together. Lester's action might be stated as "to devour her."

Script Breakdown

Title: *American Beauty*   **Character:** *Angela*

Beat:	Description:	Action:	Personalized Material
7. "...being ordinary."	Conflict	To take her	
8. "on the lips."	Operative	To devour her	

A SECRET WEAPON

Some of my clients prefer that the director not know precisely what preparation they've done for their part. Sadly, some writer-directors can get very defensive about what they feel to be a coach's invasion of their territory.

The power of Script Breakdown is in the actor's self-discovery and in the ideas the breakdown generates. Its purpose is to create ideas and choices, not to win arguments. What you learn in the Script Breakdown is your business. It is never to be shared with the director, the writer, or even the other actors in the scene. The cardinal rule of Script Breakdown is NEVER to argue a choice or dispute a director's adjustment using the language of this system. As you gain confidence and familiarity with this system, you will learn to interpret a director's adjustments in a way that's appropriate to your Preparation.

The strength of this system is in the emotional connection and the personal familiarity with the text that you'll achieve by doing the work. Even if you're not confident of your breakdown, if you do the work, you'll still know the script better and more intimately than you ever would by rote memorization.

The breakdown forces the actor to think and to imagine. It generates ideas and possibilities. These possibilities are insurance against rehearsal anxiety, out-of-continuity scheduling, and last-minute changes. Give yourself the permission to be flexible and to be imaginative. Do the breakdown just to know that you have choices. And then, as Clurman says, "burn the breakdown."

TRUTH

PART

V

THE LIFE

CHAPTER TWENTY-FOUR

ON

IMPROVISATION

I improvised, crazed by the music. Even my teeth and eyes burned
with fever. Each time I leaped I seemed to touch the sky and
when I regained earth it seemed to be mine alone.
Josephine Baker

SWING TIME

The actor has to "have a feel, a rhythm, a sense of melody and tempo," says Laurence Fishburne. "Practitioners of the craft be forewarned," he wrote in the introduction to his play *Riff Raff*. "Don't fuck around! Come correct, come to get down. A 'riff' is a 'riff.' So swing!"

Great acting swings. "The majority of musicians are interested in truth," according to tenor saxophone legend, John Coltrane. Passionate, visionary acting hits the same target as great music. It tells the truth. Coltrane's most famous recording is his cover of "My Favorite Things" from The Sound of Music.

Here's the song's melody as Rogers and Hammerstein wrote it:

And here's what Trane made out of it:

Starting with the "text" of the melody, Coltrane transformed "My Favorite Things" into an organic, vivid, and totally personal creation. He didn't just play the song; he brought it to life.

Acting has to have the same feverish, risky, seat-of-the-pants, orgasmic life as is found in a Coltrane solo. An actor, like a horn player, pours every ounce of himself, his preparation, and his technique into the piece he performs. Actors play with the text; they riff on it, and they work with and against the tempo and pitch of a scene. They'll try anything; and they'll do anything that might drop them further into the truth of their character and send that truth to the audience. Anything goes, as Coltrane says, "as long as there's some feeling of communication."

AD-LIBERATION

There is a lingering misconception that maverick writer, actor, and director John Cassavetes's films—*A Woman Under the Influence, Husbands, Faces,* and *Opening Night*—were freely improvised on the spot. The truth is that every ragged, unmistakably truthful moment in Cassavetes's films was carefully scripted. His cast was encouraged to ad-lib on-screen and improvise in rehearsal, but always within the confines of the scene as it was written in the script. There has to be a melody or a chord progression for the musician to play against. Unstructured improvisation is no more useful for an actor than it is for a musician. The actor has to have a text or some agreed-upon structure to a scene before improvising.

In improvisation, the actor goes beyond the limits of the writer's words using knowledge of the character and familiarity with the text as a launch pad. An improvisation is a journey: a voyage outside the mapped territory of the text. Over the course of that journey, the actor's imagination can freely summon anything from anywhere inside or anywhere else. Improvising can yield facts that increase an actor's understanding of the character. It can generate sensations in the actor that, although not specifically spelled out in the text, focus the character in the scripted circumstances better than the actor might be able to discover through the text alone.

Structured improvisation is a tool for prying the lid off the character's world. The actor uses the improvisation to expose the corners of that world that the text does not illuminate. What come up in improvisations are potential clues and triggers that lead to deeper understandings of the facts and conflicts in the scripted work to come. Even if these clues and triggers don't tell you anything about your character, they may tell you something about yourself that will bring you closer to the story. Improvisation can cement you and your character together in a way that nothing can drive apart.

After you've broken down the text into beats, and assigned actions to those beats, set the script aside temporarily. Armed with your knowledge of the scene and its characters, use your own words and movements to communicate the feeling of the scene. Say how you feel, based on the character's circumstances that you have learned from the text. Stay truthful and open; and for a few moments, abandon the words of the text in favor of the sensations behind them. Once you go back to the script, you'll have had the vital experience of living as your character. You can then use that freedom and life to deepen the meaning and feeling of the writer's words.

Actors that are good at improvising can travel a million miles away from the script; and then, like Coltrane, return to the underlying melody of the text. Actors who struggle with improvisation merely riff on the text, treading water by substituting a word here or a word there for what's actually on the page.

Bad improvisers will just repeat phrases from the text over and over.

The real difference is in the mindset of the actor. A good improviser wants to explore his character and his world. He hungers for the pieces of truth waiting out there, beyond the author's words, that he can bring back with him to the scripted scene.

Actors who resist exploratory improvising usually don't trust their imagination. They don't feel safe without road maps of things for their characters to say. Bad improvisers scare easily, thus failing to give themselves permission to let go of the text and jam.

SUSAN BATSON

CHAPTER TWENTY-FIVE

THE
REAL WORLD

In the long history of humankind (and animal kind, too), those who
learned to collaborate and improvise most effectively have prevailed.

Charles Darwin

RESPECT

Directors like Sidney Lumet and Francis Ford Coppola have complete respect for their actors' part in shaping their vision. Lumet budgets and schedules three weeks of paid rehearsal with his principal cast. He rents a rehearsal hall, tapes off the dimensions of the various sets, and goes through the script with his cast line-by-line and step-by-step. All ideas are heard and every possibility is considered.

Coppola gathers his cast together in a mock-up of his film set. He brings props and pieces of furniture that will be used on the set itself. Coppola works thoughtfully and personally with each member of his cast. Like Lumet, he encourages the actors to explore the script. Coppola improvises unscripted scenes that refer to the biographies his actors create for their characters. This gives his cast the sensation of actual shared memories that they can recall in character.

Coppola studied theater at Hofstra before going to film school at UCLA. Lumet is the son of an actor, and came to filmmaking after starting his own theater troupe. These artists collaborate directly and generously with their casts because they understand what the actor does, and how much the actor brings. They rely on their actors to help them to refine their directing vision.

Sidney Lumet and Coppola are among the last of a dying breed. An increasing number of film and theater directors come from commercial, writing, or photography backgrounds. For a director schooled in music videos, or a self-taught independent filmmaker, what the actor does—including preparation and process—is usually a mystery.

THE BOTTOM LINE

"Filmmaking is 90 percent casting." This truism has been uttered for as long as there have been film directors. As production costs continue to skyrocket, that figure now hovers nearer 100 percent. Even the Screen Actors Guild's low-budget contract stipulates that actors must receive straight time pay for every day of rehearsal. Whether a 100-million-dollar movie or a 1.2-million-dollar movie, producers simply won't pay for rehearsals. Theater producers are under the same financial pressures as film producers. They will not pay for anything more than a bare minimum of rehearsal.

Stanley Kubrick was notorious for shooting as many as fifty or sixty takes of any given shot. "When I have to shoot a very large number of takes, it's invariably because the actors don't know their lines, or don't know them well enough," he once said in an interview. Kubrick considered every take a filmed rehearsal. And he expected his cast to be prepared to show him something different about their character in each take. A responsible actor should approach every job he books as if it were a Kubrick film. Every actor should come to every job ready with as many different answers and ideas as can be found. Your preparation—research, exercises, the Script Breakdown itself—is all for the sake of the director's vision.

THE AUDITION

In an audition, casting agents and directors want what any audience wants—life, magic, creation—in a word, truth. If you can hold their attention, they'll give you a chance to hold an audience's attention. They want to see *something*. Bring them something, and they'll give you something in return. The actor must walk into a casting session knowing that he will make an indispensable contribution to the project. You must "bring to bright ignition that spark in every human being that longs for the miracle of transformation," as Edward G. Robinson once put it. But you have to want to make that contribution. You have to be confident that you are capable of acting that "takes us into the wilderness of human nature and leaves us there," in the words of

Tilda Swinton. Your preparation makes that confidence, and therefore that contribution, possible.

An actor who has identified and explored the *Need, Public Persona*, and *Tragic Flaw* of a character; who has established parallels through Sense Memory and Personalization; who has explored Place of Defeat, Animal Work, and the Character Private Moment; and who has thoroughly broken down the script, brings a unique presence into an audition. The actor who has invested every ounce of his soul and every waking moment in his preparation is better equipped to make that "something else" take place.

Most actors don't have much time to prepare for an audition. But even if you have less than an hour in which to get ready, you can still bring magic in with you. Simply find a truth that you wish to tell. The truth that you can connect to in the script is what will carry you through. Know what is true about the text for you. If you have that, you hold the key to the audition.

THE REHEARSAL

On many films and most plays, the actor will get one or two days to do a table read, in which the entire cast sits down together and casually reads through the script. What used to be an introductory rehearsal is rapidly becoming the only rehearsal before the actor arrives on set. It's important to make the most of the table read.

When Sam Peckinpah was preparing to shoot his revolutionary 1968 western, *The Wild Bunch*, he hadn't made a film for several years. His casting process had been difficult.

Actor after actor passed on *The Wild Bunch* script. When he finally assembled his ensemble cast for their first table read, Peckinpah was worried that the combination of actors he had gathered might not jell to bring the script to life. "The crew was there too," *Wild Bunch* actor Bo Hopkins remembered. "It was pretty well organized." Like so many anxious directors before and since, Peckinpah went into the table read wanting to be reassured that he'd made the right casting choices. Peckinpah took a seat at the head of the table, made introductions between actors and crew, and reminded his cast to relax and to read from the script informally. Everyone assembled took a breath, and opened their scripts to Page One.

As the reading began, Peckinpah saw that something wasn't working. Cast as Sykes, a grizzled, half-mad old prospector, Edmond O'Brien, a brilliant veteran character actor chosen for his versatility, read from the script as if it were a phone book. O'Brien, Hopkins recalled, "was just reading his part. No expression. He was practically mumbling." Leery of going back to the casting drawing board, Peckinpah stopped the reading and said to O'Brien, "Eddie, what are you planning on doing?"

"Oh, you mean how am I going to do the character?" O'Brien replied. "Did you want to see that now?"

"I'd like to see *some* of it now," Peckinpah said testily. As soon as the reading resumed, Edmond O'Brien leapt up and danced around the room, cackling away as Sykes. A greatly relieved Sam Peckinpah laughed and said, "Okay, I got you. You got it."

Directors often claim that they don't want their cast to "act" during a table read. But what they really mean is that they want to hear and see the character, not the actor. An actor has to arrive at the table read prepared to do one thing—make conversation. Your character must be able to make conversation with the other characters through the words of the text. That's what directors mean by "Don't act," "Read the script flat," and the various other misleading clichés they will say to actors around the table. Make sure to listen, talk, and listen as your character. Engage the other characters in conversation. That's all the actor has to do at a table read—*make conversation.*

When it comes time to get on your feet and block a scene—to work out the actual details of how the actors and the camera will move through the script—an actor-friendly director will let the actors try out movements and crosses, and find their own way through the scene; and then, fine-tune the actors' blocking along the way. More likely, the director will have everything worked out on paper, in a shot list or a storyboard. These directors will expect you to hit marks on specific lines, pick up props, and do other mechanical bits of business at a specific speed and in a specific order.

Either way, the burden of keeping track of all the cues, timings, and movements is on the actor. And a heavy burden it is! At rehearsal, take a pen and note every position and move alongside the appropriate stage direction and dialogue in your script. Wherever your character moves, what lines it moves on, what it picks up, puts down, carries, holds, or acknowledges—all get jotted down in your script in minute detail.

Then, after rehearsal is over, the real work begins. Privately, and on your own time, you, the actor, have to justify every movement, every gesture, every bit of business for your character. You must have a reason and an answer for everything your character does in a scene. You have to make everything that's happening to your character—the movement, the blocking, the physical business—ring completely true for yourself, so that it'll ring true for an audience.

The director is not there to give acting lessons; and the actor is not there to give directing pointers. The writer is probably not there at all. Acting in the real world requires that, through your own private preparation, you have already spent time in the character's head, the writer's head, and the director's head working out any questions, and clarifying and justifying your part before you arrive on set.

There is a reason and a justification for everything you do as an actor. But the only sure place where you the actor can expect to find the answer is inside yourself. You're crossing from the couch to the bar and delivering your line as you pick up a glass? Why? If you have done the research, the personal and character exploration, and the Script Breakdown, you will answer that question for yourself. You can, if necessary, answer that question fifty or sixty different ways. Want to know why you're stopping on a specific mark on a specific line? *You* supply the justification. And if you can't find anything deeper, your justification is that you came in to the audition so prepared that they hired you. It's now your job. You are being paid. "Hit the mark, look the other fellow in the eye, and tell the truth."

CHAPTER TWENTY-SIX

GOLD DUST

Acting is like peeling an onion.
You have to peel away each layer to reveal another.
Juliette Binoche

Once a week, I hold a master class called Gold Dust in which experienced actors workshop and develop characters in a group environment. Over the last few years, one of the occasional participants in these groups has been Juliette Binoche. I first met this remarkable artist when she was preparing to appear in Harold Pinter's *Betrayal* on Broadway in 2000. We've worked together several times since, and have become close friends. Binoche is the daughter of an acting teacher. She's an Academy Award winner, and an artist of unwavering commitment and intelligence. Juliette Binoche is uniquely qualified to discuss my process, the actor's responsibility, and the art form of acting.

BINOCHE ON BATSON

NEED - PUBLIC PERSONA - TRAGIC FLAW

Need, *Public Persona*, and *Tragic Flaw* are the ABCs of the actor's work. They are what scales are for the pianist; *les escalades*, as we say in French. They are a beautiful tool with which to play feelings or thoughts, and to bring life into a character even when it seems impossible to do so. *Need*, *Public Persona*, and *Tragic Flaw* let you physically become the character and tell the story. Knowing them and using them as a foundation for a character is the least an actor can do.

When I made the film *Rendez-Vous*, one of my first big roles, I was twenty years old. Back then, I intuitively created a parallel life between myself and my character. I created the character using things inside myself, because I had no other way. You might say I was my own Actor's Studio. In the films I make now, the themes are often very big. My acting choices have to reflect those themes. The characters have become more difficult and more demanding. I have to find a way to keep from losing myself or hurting myself while staying in the work. I've found that the further I go in movies, the more I have to use these three dimensions of *Need*, *Public Persona*, and *Tragic Flaw*.

I go into these roles with the courage of knowing I have a solid base. It's like a cat. A cat will throw itself out of a five-story window but then land on its legs because it has an inner equilibrium. The system of *Need*, *Public Persona*, and *Tragic*

Flaw is that equilibrium for me. At the same time that it provides a base, it keeps the work new. Even though Susan and I have gone through these three dimensions for each role, it's never felt as if we've repeated the same way of working.

BY ANY MEANS NECESSARY

The preparation we do allows me to work in very different styles of films. Comedies, political films, thrillers—they all demand very different ways of working. We've worked on Animal, for instance, more for some films and less for others. We usually have at most only a couple of weeks to prepare. As we work together, any kind of conversation is allowed. Because of the time element, our work is very condensed. It's concentrated—we share a lot of laughs and tears. We've both learned a lot more about life by doing the work we do together.

When I've done the work and am prepared, I can see a unity in my part that helps the whole dynamic of the movie. When I'm on set, all that preparation we've done makes me want to give more. I feel directly responsible for the movie in the same way that its director feels responsible for it.

In our work together for *In My Country*, Susan and I dove into apartheid. It was such a horrible experience—physically unbearable. Even today, just talking about it is unbearable. But as an actor, I have to make those difficult choices in order to participate. I want to create, and I hopefully want to change things. I believe in transformation, in life, and in changing people's consciousness through art. And changing the world for the better starts with changing people's consciousness.

TRUTH

When you haven't lived through war like my character Amira did in *Breaking and Entering*, the least you can do is learn everything you can find out about war, and try to explore war's depth and damage within yourself. You know going into that kind of a role that it's going to be terrible. You know you're going to hurt yourself. Of course, you could stop and pull back and protect a little bit of yourself; but you have to be responsible for the character and for the story. It's not masochism. I need to know these terrible things in order to give everything that I have to give to the story.

On *The Lovers on the Bridge*, in which I played a woman who lives on the street, I went out into the streets of Paris. I had to have the experience of being outside with nothing, completely on my own, in order to give everything I could to the movie. There's a knowledge that comes from those sensations and that comes from that experience. Of course, you can talk to people and see their pain and all that; but actual experience makes things more real.

RESEARCH—BUT PERSONALIZE

The films I do always contain something that is deeply rooted within me. Part of the process becomes discovering why I need to tell this particular story. I may not know why that is at first, so the film becomes a journey to find out what that connection is. For example, Amira in *Breaking and Entering* is a refugee—a single mother fleeing the Balkans with her son. She becomes a tailor in her adopted country. It happens that my grandmother, on my mother's side, was a Polish refugee during the Second World War. My grandmother came to France alone with two children; and, like Amira, she was a tailor.

I felt so much connection to Amira. I have a son, and he's almost a teenager, like Amira's son in *Breaking and Entering*, so that relationship was already there for me. A lot of things in that film were related to my Polish roots—an immigrant's roots. That was a lot to take on. But that deep connection, that truth, enables you to work so specifically that the story becomes universal. The more specific and personal you are in your work, the wider the work will be understood.

THE WORK

The things you learn have to go back into your character. You're plunging in—learning and reading, doing research, watching tapes, meeting people, and traveling. You're working on the Animal, the *Tragic Flaw*, and the Private Moment. But in the end, everything has to be forgotten. As Susan says, "You've got to burn the script and then fly." We don't really burn the script, but there is something from the preparation that has to be forgotten in order to bring the best work to it. I think of it as burning myself inside.

The trick is to tap in to yourself without knowing it. The miracle happens when you forget yourself. The ego goes away. The work shouldn't feel like work. If you're too aware of the action, if you're too aware of how you're moving, if you're too aware of what people think about you and their perceptions, then it's all gone. The work becomes self-conscious, and it loses its power as a form of art.

Part of my preparation for the film *Mary* involved immersing myself in the Gospel of Mary Magdalene. In it, Mary talks about the soul going through different stages and levels of humanness. As I read it, I thought, *Wow, this really describes acting.* When you're acting, you're going through a lot of different levels. You have to link everything in order to become fully in the work, in the art form. That's difficult for people to understand. Maybe it's better that people don't understand it. You can't understand while you're doing it, because the work happens as a sensation—an awareness. That's why acting is so fascinating: because it symbolizes all those other kinds of transformation.

SCRIPT BREAKDOWN

I know how to break down a script, but Susan usually breaks my script down for me. She really sees the different beats—Operative, Exposition, Statement of Conflict, Statement of Need, and Character Statement. When I work with Susan, we develop a view of the whole movie. There's a beginning, a middle, and an end. It might not be so clear on some films, because some of them are different, but I can always see the entire picture. Sometimes I can see it even when the director doesn't see it. That's very painful, because I can't impose myself on the director's vision. I just have to pray that he's going to see it eventually.

CLASS

I can't just work on my own. Working with the class and seeing other actors going through their work feels too good to me. Having the chance to meet people helps me to keep growing throughout my life. Class helps me tremendously. It really humbles me and gets me to a neutral place that I think we all have to start from. It reminds me that we are all workers. I don't think I'm a particularly talented actress to begin with, but I've worked a lot. I gained my talent and trained myself through working. I have experience and have developed a sensibility that lets me open up. That's one of my tools.

I remember Al Pacino thanking his teachers at the Golden Globes one year. I really understood that. Your teachers really are the only witnesses to the interior work that you do. Susan's always been quite demanding, and she won't settle for shit. That's wonderful in class. Everybody else in the class tries to be polite and says their opinion; but then we get to Susan, and she says, "No, no, no! No, shit!" That is refreshing.

After all the class work in Gold Dust, I'm ready for anything the director might want, because I'm full of all the work that we've done in class. I can adapt myself to the director's needs. It's wonderful coming onto a set already prepared and ready to give.

BRINGING THE WORK

Sometimes for the first week or so of shooting, directors will be suspicious of the preparation we've done. But eventually, they just give up. They become convinced, because they love the work. They don't always know where it's coming from, but they know that they're seeing something they've never seen before.

Working with John Boorman for the first week of *In My Country*, l would want to do a second or a third take because I thought I could go further; but he would do one take, remain behind the camera, and then want to move on. It was so technical. I thought, *I can't do this. There's no way a heart can live here. Never mind, I just won't be as good as I thought I could be in the movie. I'll be good in the next one....*

But we sat down and talked together. I said to him, "John, I don't think I can work with you. I have no creative space." He was so beautiful about it. He changed completely. There was one scene where he actually asked me to do another take. That caught me completely by surprise. He asked because he knew I could go further. At the end of the shoot, he toasted me and thanked me for teaching him about acting. It was so beautiful to see a director change like that at age seventy.

On *A Few Days in September*, which is in French and in English, Susan was worried that I would close myself up when I was playing in French. Acting in French and acting in English are quite different. With the French language, there's some quality that doesn't come out in the words. French is a very strange language. The words are as clear and as cool as ice. It's beautiful, but I think there's something emotional that sometimes doesn't come through. Before we started shooting, I had a drink with the director, and I asked him if there was anything he was afraid of. It was his first movie, and he said he was afraid of his own inexperience. He asked me what I was afraid of. Was it working with a first-time director? I said, "No, not at all. I'm afraid of not daring to be upfront in French." It really was frightening for me, because the French language is my whole childhood, education, everything to me; but I wasn't sure whether I could make it work acting in French and English.

SUSAN BATSON

ADVICE TO THE YOUNG ACTOR

My advice is never to be lukewarm. Be icy or burn, but never be in the middle. But, in order to sustain the temperature, you've got to find neutrality inside of you. You need a subtle ear, a piercing eye, and the ability to breathe in everything around you. All life is movement; all art is movement. Cells are moving all the time. You have to adapt yourself all the time to what comes in your life. It means transformation. I believe that if there's a reason why we're here, it's because we've got to learn something and let what we learn transform us.

TRUTH

Truth is an infinitely small, almost imperceptible point inside of you. It's the creative place. For a woman it's her sex. There's something at that tiny point inside a woman that is the center of creation. Truth, to me, is when you go to that little point. That's what I mean by neutrality. That's where the truth can start. That little point is like being nothing; and being nothing is being everything. Everything changes around us, because of time, because of the society we live in. Everything changes. But there's something inside us, if we look, that remains intact—this tiny, little thing.

You have to allow yourself not to know, not to have to be strong, right, or correct; otherwise you can't possibly be truthful in front of the camera. If you are so full of yourself that you think that you know everything, you won't be able to channel the truth. When we were preparing *In My Country*, I said, "I don't see why my character is responsible; she did nothing wrong, she didn't kill any black man, and didn't do anything wrong, apparently."

Susan was furious. She told me, "As a human being, as an artist, you are responsible for everything!" And bit-by-bit it came. I think it was through an improvisation that I felt it. Now I know the truth. Every human being must be responsible.

FIN

Before I met Susan, as an actress I felt very alone. I'd done quite a lot of films, and I felt alone because nobody could challenge me. Directors would try to talk to me about my characters, but somehow whatever they said was always about them, not about my work. I was in a no-man's-land of truth.

I spoke to the director Michael Haneke, a director who is able to challenge me. I told him, "I'd like the freedom to be bad and to be good in my work. I need a creative relationship that is honest about the work. I'm really looking for somebody I can talk to, somebody with whom I can be myself—someone who doesn't try to make me happy."

And he told me, "Well, you've got to meet Susan Batson. She's the only one I can think of. She's a genius." And Michael— my God, if he was saying someone was a genius... I came to New York a few months later when I was offered the play *Betrayal*. I was really looking forward to meeting Susan.

We've worked so closely ever since, that she's now somebody with whom I can share inside reference points. That's so important, because this work demands so much from inside. That demand can be very frightening. You get a lot out of reaching down deep; but it takes a lot. It's very important to have people you trust and people who know the work, because they become a point of reference. I sometimes go back to specific thoughts or details that Susan and I have worked out, to things that I wrote down while we worked together, in order to center myself.

The process of acting doesn't give you much comfort. It's beautiful to watch, but it doesn't give you the comfort that you need sometimes as an artist. Knowing that Susan's there, somewhere, and that I can get ahold of her, she's like a crystal. It's beyond words—a kind of telepathy. When you put a crystal somewhere, you know it's always there. You can put your thoughts and your being with it, and you feel stronger. For me, Susan is this crystal. She's become a companion, a sister, and a mother.

CHAPTER TWENTY-SEVEN

EX-ER ACTOR

The end is in the beginning and lies far ahead.
Ralph Ellison

How do you get to Carnegie Hall? Practice.
Jane Wagner

ACTING RESPONSIBLY

The actors of ancient Greece were elite artists as important to the foundation of Western civilization as the authors, architects, and philosophers of their time. The brilliance of Greek philosophy is preserved for all time in books. The beauty of Greek art and architecture has survived in fragments and temple ruins. But the performances that were the foundations of acting are, like their performers, gone forever.

In the centuries since, acting's status as a Primary Art Form has become tarnished. The art of acting has become so sophisticated in the last two centuries that it has the appearance of reality. Great actors bring characters to such vivid life that they are themselves mistaken for their characters. Great acting looks easy; so the civilian's assumption is that anyone can do it. "Because every man, woman, and child is able to act, more or less," British stage and screen star Dame Sybil Thorndyke once observed, "I believe it is the most difficult art to achieve perfection." The work and discipline that go into the creation of character remain hidden behind the expert application of the art itself.

The real reason that acting has slipped so far down the list of Primary Art Forms is due to actors. The vast majority of actors do not uphold their responsibility to their art. Irresponsible actors *decorate* a story instead of digging in to their characters to *tell* the story. They sell their personalities rather than creating with their instruments. They memorize dialogue rather than creating human behavior. They avoid rehearsal and preparation out of a fear of not staying "real" before the camera.

There is one word that describes these actors—*amateurs.* In its original meaning, *amateur* meant "one who does something out of love." These actors love the buzz of performing, and the money and the trappings of the acting life; but they bring nothing more than a fan's passion to the table. No matter how successful they become, they remain amateurs. Passion for acting is of course required; but it's only the beginning. The true intensity of your passion for this art is measured by your commitment. And your commitment is measured solely by how much work you do.

The courage of commitment brings actors into my circle. In my circle, you create with what you have inside. You dare to fearlessly expose the truth of a raw *Need* that drives you, the *Public Persona* covering that *Need*, and the *Tragic Flaw* that flares up wherever *Need* and *Public Persona* collide. From my circle, you look at characters like Rosa Parks and Lester Burnham not as saints or pen-and-ink creations, but as real, living human beings defined by their own truths.

In acting, art and truth are the same. When you are acting truthfully—honestly filling a character with the truth of your own humanity—you are creating life out of truth. The art is in you—the artist. *You* contain all the necessary truth of sensation to make characters live and breathe.

That truth shall indeed set you free. Truth gives you the freedom to create. As long as you create truthfully, you will remain, as I like to say, "always in the art." But maintaining the truth and protecting the actor's freedom to create are a daily struggle. Compromise and disappointment can chip away at an actor's own character until the instrument loses its vulnerability and strength. You, the actor, must make yourself responsible for preserving your instrument's range and power in the same way that any artist or athlete does—through practice.

THE HILL

Chicago Bears running back Walter Payton had a passion for his chosen craft that was unmatched in the NFL. Payton had a unique genius for carrying the ball over, around, and through the opposing team's defense. His artistry on the field was unsurpassed, and his commitment both on and off the field was astonishing. Payton's preparation, his daily off-season training regimen, was more demanding than what he went through every summer in the Bears training camp. Payton made daily runs up a hill near his home in the Chicago suburbs. "The Hill" was so steep, and his runs up it so intense, that none of his teammates were able to work out alongside him two days in a row.

When he ran the Hill, Walter Payton simulated the ferocious physical challenge of being an NFL running back. The Hill's murderously steep grade made a level, 320-foot-long football field seem easy to cover in comparison. Payton's Hill was as merciless as an oncoming defensive blitz, and as cruel as a ten-below-zero game day in Green Bay, Wisconsin.

An actor who aspires to greatness has to commit with the same intensity as Walter Payton. Thus, like any other professional, you must work at your craft each and every day of the year. You have to keep your instrument's physical strength, intelligence, emotion, imagination, sensory faculties, and empathy in good working order.

I have developed a series of acting exercises, which I refer to as "Ex-Er Actor" (standing for "exercise-your actor") exercises for the actor's instrument. You can use the fifty Ex-Er Actor exercises that follow to develop and maintain connections between yourself, the character, and the text. Each Ex-Er Actor exercise contains a short text or situation defined by a simple given circumstance. The text is followed by an Emotional Flexibility exercise. The Emotional Flexibility exercise combines a Sense Memory, a Personalization, and a Sensory Condition specific to each Ex-Er Actor scenario. Use Sense Memory and Personalization to find parallels between yourself and the character in the text. The given Sensory Condition challenges you to use your imagination to share the physical truth of the story.

SUSAN BATSON

In each combination, you have fifteen minutes to break down the beats of the text and prepare yourself to communicate the words' meaning and the story. The words don't necessarily have to be spoken exactly as written, as long as you communicate their meaning.

Drop in to the character's *Need*. Recognize the *Public Persona*. Search out the *Tragic Flaw* in the monologue. The *circumstances* are given. The *conflict*, point of *crisis*, *climax*, and *conclusion* are there. Look at the text and look into yourself and communicate those five C's through the words. Analyze, explore, choose, and do. Ex-Er Actor is your scale. Ex-Er Actor is your daily workout.

Ex-Er Actor is your Hill.

EX-ER ACTOR EXERCISES

Jerry and Jules are standing in line at a cafeteria
Jules has just asked Jerry, "How's it going?
JERRY: Well... I'm running errands for a maniac who I don't even work for. I can't ask questions of my mentor without getting my head bitten off; and correct me if I'm wrong, but wasn't that you who sent me into the boss's office for some kind of nonverbal psychological torture? Because he didn't know what the hell I was doing in his office. He hadn't sent for me. That was some kind of twisted, sick, incompetent act on your part—so I think you know exactly how it's going. It's GONE!

TRUTH

<u>Emotional Flexibility exercise:</u>

1. Sense Memory of a time when you were wronged.

2. Personalization of someone who betrayed you.

3. Sensory Condition: acid taste in your mouth.

Dana, a train wreck survivor, stands before news cameras holding his/her head and trying to make sense of what has just happened.

DANA: I flew to the back, hit the back of my head... People went flying, chairs flying. Most of the people in the front car were killed. See, the driver hit the brakes and he came running back through the cars, screaming, "Hit the deck! Hit the deck!" The children were screaming and crying...I never sit in the first or last car. I guess it's a matter of luck. I'll ride the train again, I guess. They're saying eighty-three dead. What a disaster.

<u>Emotional Flexibility exercise:</u>

1. Sense Memory of a time you experienced devastation.

2. Personalization of someone you trust to explain things.

3. Sensory Condition: dull ache on the back of the head.

Jay is a homeless person on the streets of New York City.
Someone has just tossed seventy-five cents at Jay.
Jay bends down, picks up the coins, and throws them back.

JAY: What the hell do you think this is all about? Your pitiful charity? Do you think I'm on the streets so you can throw coins away and you can walk away feeling charitable? I am here as a painful reminder that the streets are paved with greed! The golden rule is an antiquated concept void of all godliness!

Emotional Flexibility exercise:

1. Sense Memory of a time when you felt deep bitterness and cynicism.
2. Personalization of someone who belittled you.
3. Sensory Condition: feeling and smelling dirty.

Terry is an actor doing a TV spot.

Terry holds up a bottle of Godiva liqueur for the camera.

Terry's been directed to say the ad copy in a seductive way.

But throughout the dialogue, Terry battles an urge to sneeze.

By the end of the speech, Terry can't hold back and sneezes violently.

TERRY: Godiva liqueur takes up where mistletoe leaves off—tell your jolly elf how to make the holidays truly delicious. Have him bring sinfully indulgent original Godiva liqueur, creamy Godiva white chocolate liqueur, or perhaps rich Godiva cappuccino liqueur. Let them inspire you!

Emotional Flexibility exercise:

1. Sense Memory of an event when you felt very sexy.
2. Personalization of someone who turns you on.
3. Sensory Condition: an itch and sneezing.

Hamlet has returned home from studying abroad to attend his father's funeral.

Hamlet discovers that his mother and his uncle are having an affair.

In the moment before the dialogue below, Hamlet's mother and uncle have urged him to go back to school.

Hamlet waits until they are out of earshot before letting loose.

TRUTH

HAMLET: Oh that this too, too solid flesh would / Melt and thaw itself into a dew. / Oh that the everlasting had not / Fixed its cannons against self-slaughter. / Oh God—God!

<u>Emotional Flexibility exercise:</u>
1. Sense Memory of a time you felt betrayed.
2. Personalization of someone who betrayed you.
3. Sensory Condition: strong disgust or revulsion.

Jackie sits with a friend in the living room having drinks.

JACKIE: I won't eat until I am famous. I'm going on a hunger strike like what's his name-Gandhi. He got famous. But I'm not going to get famous writing a book. That's ridiculous! You're lazy! What the hell would I write? All I know is show biz. All I know is people screwing their way into the movies, popping pills, and ending up in the gutter. All t know about is aging stars, hopeful whores, and cheap studs. All I know about is tits, ass, and the truth. And nobody writes a book about that.

<u>Emotional Flexibility exercise:</u>
1. Sense Memory of a time when you felt like a failure.
2. Personalization of someone you felt inferior to.
3. Sensory Condition: a slight buzz from alcohol.

Chris is winding up an AA meeting testimony.
Chris is resolved to work for hope and peace in his,/her life, but, he/she
can sill taste the pain of the past.

CHRIS: I can no longer be casual about sex. I can't ignore my responsibility to protect myself in the age of AIDS. Also, I am more aware of my feelings. I really got nervous before a date. When I feel attracted to someone new, I ask different questions now. I'm still attracted to exciting people, but the wildness that used to draw me in makes me suspicious now. I've learned how not to give them my phone number; I'm learning to make better choices. Sometimes I look to myself for companionship and comfort rather than to a lover. And I always feel the love and acceptance of all of my friends here in these rooms.

Emotional Flexibility exercise:
1. Sense Memory of a time when you felt victorious.
2. Personalization of a trusted friend or group of trusted friends.
3. Sensory Condition: Craving a drink or something else that you know is bad for you.

Tommie is in a psychiatrist's office.

Tommie's been seeing the doctor for help with anger management.

Despite working with the doctor for nine month's, Tommie's just had a bad rage episode.

This is an emergency meeting.

Tommie is tranquilized.

TOMMIE: I went to the gym—my first time ever! When I walked in, I saw this Body-Beautiful working out. I said to myself, I want that body. So, I decided to do everything that the Body-Beautiful did. Body-Beautiful squatted, I squatted. Body-Beautiful jumped on the treadmill, I ran and jumped on the treadmill. Body-Beautiful lifted weights, I found the weights. As I'm getting my weights, Body-Beautiful comes over to me and says, "Why are you following me around, imitating everything I do?" The only answer I seemed to have was to punch Body-Beautiful in the stomach with the weight I was holding. Body-Beautiful bent over in pain and collapsed. I said, "Now are you satisfied? Now I'm not doing the same thing you're doing! When you're ready, let's work out!" Then I kicked Body-Beautiful. Well, you should have seen the way people lost their minds—screaming, shouting, pulling at me—insane!

<u>Emotional Flexibility exercise:</u>

1. Sense Memory of losing control.

2. Personalization of someone you were very angry with.

3. Sensory Condition: being tranquilized or high.

Jackie is terrified of flying.
Jackie's flight has hit turbulence.
Jackie panics at first, but becomes calm after a moment.
JACKIE: "The Lord is my shepherd, I shall not want." Oh God, not now, please. This is stupid. It has been a beautiful flight so far. Oh God... "I lift my eyes to the hills—where my help comes from."

<u>Emotional Flexibility exercise:</u>

1. Sense Memory of a time you experienced terror.

2. Personalization of God

3. Sensory Condition: a cramped airplane seat.

Pat is terminally ill.

Full-blown AIDS has seized Pat's body.

Pat is seated in a chair in a hospital room talking to his/her mother.

PAT: I've seen some amazing things: war, a herd of buffaloes, ants working in their colonies. Laugh, go ahead. I've been kissed so passionately that I thought those kisses would kill me. Laugh, go ahead. I understand that it sounds so melodramatic, right? But there's more. And the most important thing: I've been visited by the presence of God and Jesus Christ; and always they whisper in my right ear, 'Do not be afraid..." So laugh, go ahead. It's a great sound. *[Pat laughs and cries]*

Emotional Flexibility exercise:

1. Sense Memory of a time when your expectations were positive; when you anticipated good.
2. Personalization of Mother.
3. Sensory Condition: a tapeworm crawling around in your body eating away all that is positive in you.

Marty is a famous rock star in his/her dressing room, complaining to his/her road manager about the accommodations.

MARTY: Val, Val, this is catastrophic! Do you see what has been placed before us here? I can't believe the disgrace. I said before we booked the place, before you made the phone calls to confirm our dates here, that there should be no green M&M's in the fucking assortment. Do you see green M&M's? Say yes, Val. There are green M&M's in the friggin' dressing room. They're like parasites! I've never been so outraged! Let me do the honor of describing your job again. You are required to oversee the finite details of what gets placed in our path at all times. I am not going to say this again. You should be ashamed. Now pick those little monsters out of there, or the band doesn't play. Jesus H. Christ! There you go. That's much better. See, I can breathe easier now. Ahhhh...

Emotional Flexibility exercise:

1. Sense Memory of a time when you acted like a baby.
2. Personalization of someone you treated horribly.
3. Sensory Condition: a bad taste.

Shelley's name has been announced as the winner of the Academy Award for Best Actor/Actress.
Shelley buried his/her father two days before the ceremony.
The combination of joy and sorrow makes Shelley feel a bit faint.
Shelley heads to the podium without any notes, and improvises an acceptance speech dedicating the award to his/her father.

Emotional Flexibility exercise:

1. Sense Memory of a great joy.
2. Personalization of someone you loved very much but lost.
3. Sensory Condition: faintness or fever.

You are soul deejay Baby Diamond, singing along with the fade-out of Al Green's "Let's Stay Together."
BABY DIAMOND: "Let's stay together, loving you whether, whether, times are good or bad, happy or sad..." Good evening, this is the sweet tones of LOVE 400 at midnight. Piloting you into those starry, starry midnight skies is yours truly, Baby Diamond.

Coming up is that classic oldie "Dedicated to the One I Love." If I may, listeners, I do have to take care of some Personal business right here and right now. Darling, I did wrong. Was a fool. I put my stupidity publicly on the airwaves. Publicly, I beg your forgiveness. You are the kindest, sweetest, the most beautiful man [woman] on the face of the earth. Baby, please come back to me. I'm a fool, baby, but please come back. THIS IS dedicated to the one I love...

Emotional Flexibility exercise:
1. Sense Memory of a time when you publicly apologized.
2. Personalization of a person whom you would do anything to keep in your life.
3. Sensory Condition: a broken heart.

Dana is on the phone with a very close friend.

DANA: So on the way to the second session, Billie is working hard to convince me that he [she] will love me to his [her] dying day. Nothing would dissuade Billie's love! I swallow it all, hook, line, and sinker. So we are in with the therapist, and I'm spilling my guts, and the therapist says, "Dana, don't you see that Billie doesn't care about your unhappiness? Isn't that right, Billie?" Wait, just wait... Billie says, "Yes!" Then the therapist—No, the therapist is only the messenger. Don't shoot the messenger. So the therapist says, "Billie can't make a commitment; isn't that right, Billie?" "Yup," Billie said—yes as clear as day! So that was the end. The whole relationship ended right then. All I can feel is pain and shock! All I've eaten since yesterday is a cup of coffee. So this evening, I thought I'd go get some food that I love to eat.

TRUTH

Who should I meet? Yes... Billie. Smiling, friendly, looking great. And me, my face all contorted, yeah, my right eye twitching. But Billie? Nothing! I am absolutely certain that Billie is insane! No, there is no other explanation!

Emotional Flexibility exercise:

1. Sense Memory of a time when you were hurt by love.
2. Personalization of someone who has hurt you and of someone who cares.
3. Sensory Condition: A twitch or tic or other physical gesture you want to hide.

Tommie is a prostitute dressing and getting ready to leave a regular client's bedroom.

The client has confessed to having feelings for Tommie.

Tommie feels the same way about the client but won't admit it.

TOMMIE: Hey, let's try one more time. I am an escort, a la-di-da word for prostitute. Hustler. My job is to make you believe in any fantasy you so desire. I made you believe you were in love with me, but I cannot fall in love with anyone. I am a whore; I want the money. I don't want the street. I was on the street at fourteen, and stayed until I got smart at eighteen. Four long years. So there is no love, no romance, just good technique.

<u>Emotional Flexibility exercise:</u>

1. Sense Memory of a time when you told a very big lie.

2. Personalization of a person you love deeply.

3. Sensory Condition: coldness.

Ronnie is talking to a reporter outside of a nursing home that is under investigation for patient abuses.

Ronnie's mother is a resident there.

RONNIE: Kerosene! Kerosene! They washed them with kerosene! It's something out of a Charles Dickens novel! But it's the year 2007; how is this possible? When I walked into my mother's room, it reeked of kerosene! Kerosene! When I asked, they said it wasn't. No, sure smelled like kerosene. To protect all the patients from lice and things. Oh, God, what do I do? This is awful! I'm my mother's only living relative, but I can't take care of her by myself. She has Alzheimer's... *[Ronnie turns and walks away]*

<u>Emotional Flexibility exercise:</u>

1. Sense Memory of a time when you witnessed something horrific.

2. Personalization of Mother when she was sick.

3. Sensory Condition: the smell of kerosene.

Tony is a songwriter with writer's block.

Tony has the first sixteen bars of a song written.

Tony sings and re-sings those first sixteen bars (use the first four to eight lines of any familiar song like "Hoppy Birthday") but can't go any further.

TRUTH

After repeating the song fragment several times, Tony sits down and stares blankly out into the world.

Finally, Tony very calmly starts the song and sings it in its entirety.

Emotional Flexibility exercise:

1. Sense Memory of a time when you felt creatively blocked.

2. Personalization of someone who inspires you.

3. Sensory Condition: a place where you felt inspired.

Cat is arguing with a roommate.

CAT: I am sick of the universe revolving around you! I seem to have no rights! I just ask that because of the condition of the place, you do not bring anyone into it; and then I am maligned and totally disrespected! You twist and distort everything I say. I don't think that it's wise to have people in here with everything falling down! Is that too much to ask? I don't want it. Right, wrong, insane, stupid, a dictator—all the million different things I am supposed to be! Forget all that. How about doing it just because I want it that way? How many things do I ask you to do because I just want them? How many? *[Cat exits]*

Emotional Flexibility exercise:

1. Sense Memory of a time when you fought for your rights.

2. Personalization of a person to whom you constantly give up your power.

3. Sensory Condition: a place you live/lived in that's a mess.

Jackie is talking to his/her lover in the bedroom.

JACKIE: I understand you! How could I not understand you? We've gone over the same stuff fifty times now! I'm in the midst of shooting a picture. Please be rational! Just let me finish the picture and we'll do it properly, I promise you. I love you, but can we just be in bed together, once, just once, without you putting your mother in the bed with us?

Emotional Flexibility exercise:

1. Sense Memory of a time when you begged someone to accept you for who you are.
2. Personalization of someone you love but who drives you crazy.
3. Sensory Condition: Anxiety attack—the feeling of bugs crawling all over your body. Endow each bug with something that makes you insecure in your life.

Dana is a nervous investor talking on a cell phone.
It's spring of 1999, just prior m the Internet stock price plunge.

DANA: Nah, man, nah. Too risky. I don't like it. I want out. It's too risky. Listen, man, we made a lot of money together on this one, but it's over. The market dropped fifteen points this week. ...Well, then, you got my blessing. I'm selling my end. This Internet business is too volatile. I'll keep my block of Microsoft, but I'm taking profits on Yahoo! and all the portal stocks. The tech bubble's gonna pop, man. ...All right, peace.

TRUTH

<u>Emotional Flexibility exercise:</u>

1. Sense Memory of a time when you panicked.

2. Personalization of someone you feel controls your life.

3. Sensory Condition: oppressive heat.

Jay is talking to himself/herself while looking in the minor and getting ready for a date.

JAY: I tell her I love her [him] because I hate her. I'm nice to her now to do her in later. Does she kiss me and pet me just to perplex me? If I cut my throat, will she aid and abet me? After she's gone, I'll quickly forget her, go on the prowl, and find something better.

<u>Emotional Flexibility exercise:</u>

1. Sense Memory of a time when you suspected you were being taken advantage of.

2. Personalization of someone from whom you want total admiration.

3. Sensory Condition: a private moment in which the personal activity is checking out your body in a mirror.

Terry is arguing with a business partner.

TERRY: One last thing: you're a Communist. No, you're a hardheaded socialist! Why can't you get the Michael Jordan theory? Why? So what if Mike is a capitalist—BE A CAPITALIST! You're running our business into the ground with your stupid socialism! Mike says, "I'm the best, so pay me the best!" He knows he's Number One. You're asking for no money from anyone like you are the worst! This is really some neurotic paradigm that I cannot be around. Think like a billionaire, or I am out of here!

Emotional Flexibility exercise:

1. Sense Memory of a time when you felt your own power and worth.
2. Personalization of someone you have a business or financial relationship with.
3. Sensory Condition: Animal Work incorporating a lion.

Sam is on the phone with his/her father.

SAM: It is haunting me and I have to leave. No, Dad. Well, I'm not as strong as you, I guess. I cannot stay. Deception, Dad! I deceived everyone. Because I wanted to be loved—rich and famous. Now I'm nothing. There is no explaining. They asked me to resign. There is no case. I did everything they say I did. Everything. I don't know, Dad. Because I don't know who I am. Being your child was not enough. I wanted to be something more than your child. Yup, I'm—I proved nothing to myself except how much shame I have in me. Shame and disgust. *[Sam's father hangs up on the other end]* Dad? ...Dad!

Emotional Flexibility exercise:

1. Sense Memory of a time you hated who you were.
2. Personalization of your father.
3. Sensory Condition: a bad smell.

Chris watches as cops search his/her bag at an airport.

CHRIS: And don't tell me to calm down. I'll calm down when you stop picking on me. I must have the look of your drug-carrying profile, but ha-ha, the joke's on you. I've never done a drug in my life, and I'm far too smart to be dealing! So when are you gonna stop being idiots and treat me not as a profile but as a human being? And I want those bags back in the same condition they were in when you opened them, and that was neat! Neat, anal neat! If they're not, then I'll be doing my own searching!

Emotional Flexibility exercise:
1. Sense Memory of a time when you were isolated.
2. Personalization of someone who has no respect for you.
3. Sensory Condition: Bugs crawling over body. Endow each bug with one of the little things in life that makes you angry.

Val has been convicted of multiple crimes.
Val is making a statement before sentence is passed.

VAL: Your Honor, this does not excuse my behavior, but it may explain it. For years, I've been in denial about this stuff. I was seven. It was Thanksgiving morning. My mother said she had to do some last minute shopping. See, my father had committed suicide on the day I was born. Mom did the best she could until that Thanksgiving Day. That morning she walked out and she never came back. I waited. Nowhere to go, no one to call. Finally, it came Monday, and I went to school. I was starving. I stank. I was like an animal. They called the authorities, and I became a state kid. I never heard from my mother again. Yes, I became a criminal. Yes, I've stolen, killed, forged—you name it. Put me in jail, throw away the key, or kill me, because I am a menace to society. I want my mommy!

Emotional Flexibility exercise:
1. Sense Memory of a time when you needed your mother and she wasn't there.
2. Personalization of someone who passed judgment on you.
3. Sensory Condition: The little boy or girl inside of you.
   What is the thing you love most about your inner child?

Pat is trying m comfort Sam, who is not feeling well.
PAT: Let me do my French toast for you. Don't make that ugly face, I make good French toast. What do you want from me? I'm not a doctor, not a therapist, what do you want me to do? Let me do my French toast. It's good—nice maple syrup, lots of butter, comfort food—it just may help. I don't know what else to do. Please stop crying. They said on the emergency room phone that you'll be fine. What do you want me to do?

Emotional Flexibility exercise:
1. Sense Memory of a time when you wanted to help but didn't know how.
2. Personalization of someone who needs your help.
3. Sensory Condition: having to go to the bathroom.

Cameron is speaking in a bereavement support group.
CAMERON: My whole family is traumatized. We try to support each other, but you know this is each person's journey. No two

people can do it the same. All of it is personal. When Billy called to borrow my car, I sensed something was wrong about it. It's ostentatious. It's a Mercedes. There've been these highway shootings, so I said maybe don't take my car. But he wanted to impress this girl—so I said, okay. But my last words were, "Billy, be careful—just be careful." It's a Mercedes sports coupe, a great show-off car. Just before he pulled out, I said, "Come on, let me rent you a car." He laughed and said he didn't know I loved him so much, and then he sped away... I know we say here we have to go through the pain. This is the second anniversary of his death, and I'm saying the same things I said when the cops called and told me someone shot him on the freeway while he was changing a tire. Hello—the killer is in jail for life, the key's thrown away. And I'm in hell, still wondering why I gave him the car keys. Why didn't I throw myself in front of the car? Why not me? Let me be dead!

Emotional Flexibility exercise:

1. Sense Memory of a time you felt very guilty.

2. Personalization of someone you've lost.

3. Sensory Condition: a heavy weight on your chest.

Nick is an actor shooting an instant coffee commercial.
When Nick opens the prop jar of coffee, the smell is disgusting.
NICK: Open up and smell our golden aroma. *[Opens up the jar but it stinks. Nick covers up with a big smile]* Smell our golden aroma and prepare yourself for an extrasensory experience.

<u>Emotional Flexibility exercise:</u>

1. Sense Memory of a time when you are forced to do something you don't want to do.
2. Personalization of someone who put pressure on you.
3. Sensory Condition: a horrible smell.

Bobby has just received a hand transplant.

Bobby cradles his/her new hand and addresses reporters at a press conference.

BOBBY: Very briefly, I'm pleased. I don't know if you can imagine being the first person to have a hand transplant. It is beyond awesome. I am trying to accept this miraculous scientific process, because I do want a hand, I really do! Finally, I wish to thank the amazing doctors—especially Dr. Jones. Also the sweetest, kindest nurse staff; and there are no words for my incredible family. Thank you.

<u>Emotional Flexibility exercise:</u>

1. Sense Memory of a time when you achieved something very special.
2. Personalization of a person who has helped you very much.
3. Sensory Condition: holding a newborn baby.

Charlie is a musician on a talk show.

Charlie has been asked about his/her reputation for being difficult.

CHARLIE: I guess I am difficult. You hear it all the time, so okay, I'm difficult. What can I do? I just do my music, every day,

365 days a year. I wouldn't change anything—it all has made me who I am today—"difficult" and all. Uh-oh, umm, I must say finally that not once have I compromised. I know all the people I've worked with—engineers and all—say that I am a pain in the ass. Okay, this may be true—but I know I am a nice person. It hurts to be seen like that. *[Tears well up]* Damn, what a wuss thing to do! Where did that come from?

Emotional Flexibility exercise:

1. Sense Memory of a time when you made an honest confession about yourself.
2. Personalization of a person who has found you trying or problematic.
3. Sensory Condition: warm arms embracing you.

Sal is on the phone after being stood up by a lover.

SAL: What happened last night? I came by, but you weren't home. I thought that was supposed to be over. Yes, I did. I distinctly said tomorrow night, and that was two days ago. Anyway, I'm having dinner with my parents tonight. You up for it? But you just said you thought tonight was our night. Oh—I guess that's more important. It's all right. Is everything okay, babe? Things haven't felt the same, lately. Sure, I understand. I don't want to interfere with the case of the century... No sarcasm and no sexism. Yeah, right. Love you too. *[Sal hangs up the phone]* Jesus! Something's rotten on Central Park West!

Emotional Flexibility exercise:

1. Sense Memory of a time when someone lied to you.

2. Personalization of someone you love.

3. Sensory Condition: Slimy worms crawling all over your body. Each worm is a doubt.

Struggling with an outrageous hangover, Jackie barely manages to answer the phone.

JACKIE: Yeah? Shut up! Whisper! What? What's wrong is, did you know that a hangover is not having enough water in your body to run your Krebs cycle? Which is exactly what happens when you die of thirst. So, yes, dying of thirst would feel like the hangover that finally kills you. *[Jackie hangs up the phone and lies down on the floor like a dead person]*

Emotional Flexibility exercise:

1. Sense Memory of a time when you felt like death warmed over.

2. Personalization of someone who gives you a headache.

3. Sensory Condition: headache and cottonmouth.

Sammy is talking to a clerk at a U.S. consulate passport and visa office.

SAMMY: See, you're just obsessing over the details. You're completely missing the big picture. First, the fact that the bitch [bastard]—the so-called person—had a prior marriage is a big shock to me. I'm sure more of a shock to me than the Swiss government. Look, she [he] totally burned me. She took my money, $4,000 to be exact. She totally lied to me. And then this husband, this prior spouse, starts calling everyone and making all this noise. So, *you* tell me what the hell I should do!

Emotional Flexibility exercise:
1. Sense Memory of a time in your life when you felt wronged.
2. Personalization of someone who has stolen from you or used you.
3. Sensory Condition: nerves on end-bugs crawling on you.

Terry's boss has offered Terry a settlement for sexual harassment.
TERRY: You did come on to me, and no, I intend to do nothing about it. I want your admission, and this cute little package of money—of cash. What is it? A couple of thousand? Give me a million or nothing at all. That's right, a couple thousand will only make me feel like a slime ball like you! For the last time, you did come on to me. Your silence indicates to me that you intend to only slip me an envelope of money and refuse to express any real contrition for your actions. So I'm just gonna let you keep your few thousands, and you won't be hearing from my lawyer. I'm staying right here in the company; and every day you'll ask yourself what it is that I want. Adios, amigo.

Emotional Flexibility exercise:

1. Sense Memory of a time when you stood up for yourself.
2. Personalization of someone who violated you.
3. Sensory Condition: Animal Work—a fox.

Maxie is a drunk driver on the witness stand.

MAXIE: So when the call came that my son had set fire to his mattress, I ran out of the bar. I remember hearing the bartender say maybe I shouldn't drive, that I'd had too much to drink. But all I could think about was Mikey. He's only four years old. I pushed the gas pedal to the floor, screaming all the way! The next thing I remember is waking up in the hospital screaming about my son. I was told he was fine, and that I had struck and killed two people. My son is fine, I am in hell, and two people are dead. Justice? There is no justice! My son has no father [mother]! That couple, so young, has no life! Just kill me! Nothing makes sense!

Emotional Flexibility exercise:

1. Sense Memory of a time when you did wrong.
2. Personalization of someone you don't want anything to happen to.
3. Sensory Condition: bad taste and something that you hate about yourself.

Pat is on the phone with his/her agent, enraged.

PAT: Apparently they had too many drinks between the matinee and the evening performance. So first, Richardson comes reeling onto the stage. I run over to help him and he yanks his arm away from me, goes to the apron of the stage, breaks the fourth wall, and says to the audience, "If you think I'm a mess, you haven't seen nothing yet!" I run to the wings to see what the stage manager is going to do. The other drunk idiot attacks me, or should I say molests. Gay, straight, what the hell does it matter? My clothes are being ripped off; I'm being kissed and humped. I'm screaming for dear life! Richardson laughs so hard he falls off the stage, and the audience gives us a standing ovation!

Emotional Flexibility exercise:
1. Sense Memory of a time when you were humiliated.
2. Personalization of a person you seek help or guidance from.
3. Sensory Condition: the smell of booze on someone's breath.

Lindsay is doing some damage control.

LINDSAY: So how long is this going to go on? Or do you plan never to speak to me again? Look, you know I have a big mouth. I don't have a built-in filter. I wasn't raised in gentile society. Where I come from you call it like you see it! And yeah, I'll say it a thousand times, I think circumcision is a cruel and barbaric practice! Okay, so maybe I shouldn't have said it just as the rabbi was about to start the process; but it did shake things up. Right. Your sister got like, "Are you going to hurt my child?" Yeah, it hurts. Hey, hey, wait, where you going?

Emotional Flexibility exercise:

1. Sense Memory of a time when you were sure you were right.
2. Personalization of someone you want on your side.
3. Sensory Condition: excruciating pain.

Sal is being interviewed for Sports illustrated.

SAL: Absolutely not. I would not encourage my child to play tennis. Absolutely not! I'm not going to defend the tennis circuit. Yeah, it looks all civilized and proper, but it is a cutthroat business. If I sound a little bitter, well, I stupidly thought the sport of tennis would look after me. I was so wrong. It's a game of me against them, not like football with a team and all! Look, I was the youngest player to win the Davis Cup, then I won Wimbledon, and then I got injured, then I got out. I like commenting on the game—especially Wimbledon—but I'm not going to lie and tell you the tennis world is a nice place.

Emotional Flexibility exercise:

1. Sense Memory of a bitter experience doing something you love to do.
2. Personalization of someone who took the joy out of your dream.
3. Sensory Condition: a bad taste.

A couple shop for wedding rings at Tiffany's.

JACKIE: We said we weren't going to spend a fortune on rings. We said we'd share the cost, spend little, and have fun hanging out in Tiffany's. This is turning out to be not fun, no fun. And don't shush me! You know I got a New York mentality. I am a renter, not a buyer! I can't make big purchases; it freaks me out! I swear to God I feel like I'm going to... *[Jackie starts to cry and runs out of the store]*

Emotional Flexibility exercise:

1. Sense Memory of a time when you felt forced to do something against your will.
2. Personalization of someone you would like to be with for the rest of your life.
3. Sensory Condition: a deep aversion.

A French spectator is interviewed by American television at the Tour de France.

SPECTATOR: No, no, keep the camera on me, because I am the only French person who will praise Lance Armstrong. He is in the same category as Michael Jordan and Tiger Woods. No other French person will say that. Most French people think he isn't true about his illness. Can you believe that? *Je ne sais pas...* One last word—I hope to see him next year!

Emotional Flexibility exercise:

1. Sense Memory of a time when you were in awe of someone.
2. Personalization of someone to whom you want to prove something.
3. Sensory Condition: fighting to be heard over a crowd and commotion.

Sam is having a lovers' quarrel.

SAM: This is not my artist's bullshit! I do absolutely identify with people. In fact, I will go so far as to say that is my talent. The hell with you! Go ahead—roll your eyes! It is my talent! I get so identified with people that I feel frightened when I separate from them. Call it psychotic, but this is how I feel. I have no self. I've gone into that person, and I get things from that that not too many people, or not too many artists, get. Even in those moments, I overcome alienation. It's my ticket to reality! So, don't accuse me of codependency. We are talking talent when we speak of me! Bye, darling—what a pity we couldn't share the same space!

Emotional Flexibility exercise:

1. Sense Memory of a hostile breakup.
2. Personalization of someone you want to be very intimate with.
3. Sensory Condition: feeling ridiculed-egg on the face.

Danny is ordering room service from an operator who doesn't speak English.

DANNY: Room service? Yes, this is room 337. Yes, please. The grilled salmon but no sauce. No sauce, please. *Comprendo?* No, no sauce. No, none, *nada.* Yes, no sauce, gravy, dressing! *Nada!* Nothing on the salmon. *Nada* on it! *Si, si, si!* Um, yes, coffee, just plain American. *Americano, si.* Only whole grain bread. Rolls, whole grain, whole wheat. No, just brown bread. No white bread. No, no white, brown! *Si! Si!* Thank you! [*Danny hangs up the phone*]

TRUTH

Emotional Flexibility exercise:

1. Sense Memory of a time when you felt totally misunderstood.

2. Personalization of someone who won't listen to you.

3. Sensory Condition: feeling stupid.

Sisgo, a leather-clad pop star, pontificates on a talk show.

SISGO: That's not fair, Jay. Look, I stay away from all that negative stuff. I'm not really into the male-bashing and the female-bashing thing. Look, I think—here is a way to say something if something is messed up—you know what I mean? Like, look, it's messed up, said just that simple. Like, if it's tight, it's tight. Jay, just call me old-fashioned. In all this leather, I'm very simple. Like I have a really, really tight relationship with God. I leave almost everything in my life to divine intervention. *[The audience claps, and Sisgo applauds them back]*

Emotional Flexibility exercise:

1. Sense Memory of a time when you were the center of attention.

2. Personalization of someone you feel you must convince who you are.

3. Sensory Condition: a positive thing you feel about yourself.

Tony introduces a candidate from a podium at a huge political convention.

TONY: My fellow Americans, I stand before you, the child of one of the most brilliant political minds in the world. I stand before you, the child of the man who disgraced himself in front of the entire world. I stand before you, the child of the woman who loves this man for better or for worse. I stand before you, the child who has learned to forgive my father. I stand before you, totally at peace with my forgiveness; and I stand before you, pleading with you to do as I have done, and not to impede the success of this party by clinging to errors of human weakness, but instead cling to those brilliant accomplishments of the human mind, soul, and heart. Thank you! God bless!

Emotional Flexibility exercise:
1. Sense Memory of a time when you fought for something you believed in.
2. Personalization of someone you love who's been vilified and that you have forgiven.
3. Sensory Condition: place—an enormous, echoing auditorium.

A baseball team owner addresses his/her team in the locker room.

OWNER: You ask me what will satisfy me. The best! I am quite satisfied with the best! I am quite satisfied with the best ballplayers, the best team, and the best effort from that team every game! The best! So, this was not the best game you ever played! In fact, this was a crap gamer a no-brainer game. Now, I know you look at me and probably have decided that I am too young to know what I'm talking about. Too young, too everything! Well, let me tell you something. As you factor in the thing about me not knowing anything, factor in that I'm the one who pays you. I sign the checks. I own the team. I know everything, and I know what I want. I want the best! If I think you're not the best, all you can look forward to is your ass kissing the pavement outside this stadium!

Emotional Flexibility exercise:

1. Sense Memory of a time when you felt betrayed.

2. Personalization of someone who has disappointed you.

3. Sensory Condition: Animal Work—a caged lion.

Chris has agreed to wed Ronnie.

CHRIS: I can't believe it's going to happen. Really, I'm not sure I'm worthy of you. I don't know if I'll ever be good enough for you. I don't know if I'll be able to give to you as much as you've given me, but I'll try, I really will. I'll try. *[Pause]* Damn! That was the worst insecurity attack! Can you imagine? Me feeling not worthy of you! Damn, I must be crazy!

Emotional Flexibility exercise:

1. Sense Memory of a time when you exposed a deep insecurity.

2. Personalization of someone you love.

3. Sensory Condition: your greatest insecurity about yourself and your greatest insecurity about your body.

Dana has just shown his/her latest masterpiece to a close friend.

DANA: You come into my home, and you look at my new painting; you make a face of absolute disdain, and then you have the nerve to ask me, "What is this infantile scribble?" Well, for your infantile, ignorant information, this is the work of a modern Native American artist. It's a testament to ancestral truths that stretch back to the beginning of time. This is a collector's piece of work! I don't know how you can look at this work and not know that it has the answers you seek. Why am I talking to you? And I sure as hell know I'm not sleeping with you; so find your way to the door. And this is nonadjustable and nonnegotiable. Good night!

Emotional Flexibility exercise:

1. Sense Memory of a time when someone angered you to the brink of violence.
2. Personalization of someone you find to be uncultured but a physical turn-on.
3. Sensory Condition: the vision of an extraordinary piece of art.

Val and Tony are at odds over Tony's addictions.

VAL: Read my lips, Tony—we cannot cover a $100,000 bet! A horse head in our beds won't be nothing compared to what they'll do to us! Look, I know you want it all, and you want it fast—fast cars, a house, lots of clothes—You want it now! Because Tony, you got a problem. You're a cokehead. You are an addict! Now, because I love you, you got two choices, only two.

One—get out of my life now, and never, ever look back. Or, two, take this envelope. Inside is a plane ticket to a place in Arizona, a rehab center. Also enclosed is a check written out to the center and some petty cash for cab fare to and from the airport. So what will it be?

Emotional Flexibility exercise:

1. Sense Memory of a time when you knew you had to let go of a friend.
2. Personalization of an addictive person.
3. Sensory Condition: fear.

Charlie, a reporter, meets with his/her newspaper's lawyer.
CHARLIE: Prove I'm right? Can I prove it? No. I don't have to, do I? Look, I wrote what I heard from my source. I never claimed it was anything else. What the hell do you want from me? I'm not the lawyer, you are! If you thought I was on shaky ground, why did you approve the story? Look, if the paper killed every story you thought was libelous, there wouldn't be a paper! Listen closely: I stand behind what I wrote.

Emotional Flexibility exercise:

1. Sense Memory of a time when you fought for something you believed in.
2. Personalization of someone who has blocked you.
3. Sensory Condition: acid taste in mouth.

Ronnie confesses to the police.

RONNIE: I *am* cooperating. Damn! It's simple: look, on Thursdays or Fridays. You'll see two people, usually a birdie and a dude, two of them leaving the bank. Two of them means a couple of grand. Like I said, we don't use guns, just a knife! Those other robberies were not us. We don't use guns. The knife does fine. All we do is follow them back to their office or factory, and when they're getting out of the car, we grab the one with the money. Knife to the throat makes them real scared. They drop the money, we scoop it up, hold on to the person to the last second, and we're off. No one is shot. I ain't in that real kind of violent league.

<u>Emotional Flexibility exercise:</u>
1. Sense Memory of a time when you told a horrible truth about yourself.
2. Personalization of someone who is always judging you.
3. Sensory Condition: fear.

THE END

Do you remember Sean Dean, that actor from the circle with a huge emotional life? He died not so long ago. I thought he had the talent to make him a legend. I mourn Sean and Mercedes and all the other young actors who pass before they can realize their dreams. They are killed by bullets and many

TRUTH

demons that exist in our society. Perhaps because of their youthfulness, they seem to live on for me. I see them in a stage or screen moment or in the sparkling eyes of a passionate new student. It could be that I can't let go of their beauty, dreams, and passion—their search for truth has touched me too deeply to forget.

SUSAN BATSON

SELECTED BIBLIOGRAPHY

Fishburne, Laurence. *Riff Raff*. New York: Dramatist's Play Service, 1997.

Hagen, Uta (with Haskell Frankel). *Respect for Acting*. New York: Wiley, 1973.

Hagen, Uta. *A Challenge for the Actor*. New York: Scribner, 1991

Hansberry, Lorraine. *A Raisin in the Sun*. New York: Random House, 1995.

Kazan, Elia. *Elia Kazan: A Life*. New York: Da Capo, 1997.

Le Gallienne, Eva. *The Mystic in the Theater Eleonora Duse*. New York: Arturo's, 1973.

McKee, Robert. *Story: Substance' Structure' Style and the Principles of Screenwriting*. New York: ReganBooks, 1997.

Miller, Alice. *The Drama of the Gifted Child*. New York: Basic Books, 1996.

Olivier, Laurence. *Confessions of an Actor*. New York: Orion, 1994.

Olivier, Laurence. *On Acting*. New York: Simon & Schuster 1987.

O'Neal, Tatum. *A Paper Life*. New York: Harper, 2004.

Parks, Rosa and Jim Haskins. *Rosa Parks: My Story*. New York: Puffin, 1999.

Parks, Rosa. *Quiet Strength*. New York: Zondervan, 2000.

Sheehy, Helen. *Eleonora Duse: A Biography*. New York: Knopf, 2003.

Stanislavski, Konstantin. *An Actor Prepares*. New York: Rutledge, 1964.

Strasberg, Lee. *A Dream of Passion: The Development of the Method*. New York: Penguin, 1987.

Wallach, Eli. *The Good, the Bad, and Me*. New York: Harcourt, 2005.

Weddle, David. *"If They Move...Kill 'Em! "*: *the Life and Times of Sam Peckinpah*. New York: Grove, 1994.

FILMOGRAPHY

A partial list of films cited or used as examples

AMERICAN BEAUTY (1999)
Dir. Sam Mendes

THE AVIATOR (2004)
Dir. Martin Scorsese

BABY DOLL (1956)
Dir. Elia Kazan

THE BOURNE IDENTITY (2002)
Dir. Doug Liman

BREAKING AND ENTERING (2006)
Dir. Anthony Minghella

BRINGING UP BABY (1938)
Dir. Howard Hawks

BROKEBACK MOUNTAIN (2005)
Dir. Ang Lee

THE CAINE MUTINY (1954)
Dir. Edward Dmytryk

CAPE FEAR (1991)
Dir. Martin Scorsese

CAPOTE (2005)
Dir. Bennett Miller

CASABLANCA (1942)
Dir. Michael Curtis

CATCH ME IF YOU CAN (2002)
Dir. Steven Spielberg

THE CONTENDER (2000)
Dir. Rod Lurie

CRASH (2004)
Dir. Paul Haggis

DEEP IMPACT (1998)
Dir. Mimi Leder

DOG DAY AFTERNOON (1975)
Dir. Sidney Lumet

EASY RIDER (1969)
Dir. Dennis Hopper

ETERNAL SUNSHINE OF THE SPOTLESS MIND (2004)
Dir. Michel Gondry

EYES ON THE PRIZE (1987)
Dir. Henry Hampton

EYES WIDE SHUT (1999)
Dir. Stanley Kubrick

FACES (1968)
Dir. John Cassavetes

FAR FROM HEAVEN (2002)
Dir. Todd Haynes

FIGHT CLUB (1999)
Dir. David Fincher

TRUTH

FIVE EASY PIECES (1970)
Dir. Bob Abelson

FORREST GUMP (1994)
Dir. Robert Zemeckis

FRANCES (1982)
Dir. Graeme Clifford

THE FRENCH CONNECTION (1971)
Dir. William Friedkin

GIRL, INTERRUPTED (1999)
Dir. James Mangold

GLORY (1989)
Dir. Edward Zwick

THE GODFATHER (1972)
Dir. Francis Ford Coppola

THE GODFATHER: PART II (1974)
Dir. Francis Ford Coppola

GOING IN STYLE (1979)
Dir. Martin Brest

GONE WITH THE WIND (1939)
Dir. Victor Fleming

HE GOT GAME (1998)
Dir. Spike Lee

THE HUNCHBACK OF NOTRE DAME (1923)
Dir. Wallace Worley

HUSBANDS (1970)
Dir. John Cassavetes

SUSAN BATSON

HUSTLE & FLOW (2005)
Dir. Craig Brewer

IN MY COUNTRY (2004)
Dir. John Bormann

THE INSIDER (1999)
Dir. Michael Mann

I THINK I LOVE MY WIFE (2007)
Dir. Chris Rock

JET LAG (2002)
Dir. Danièle Thompson

KEANE (2004)
Dir. Lodge H. Kerrigan

LADY SINGS THE BLUES (1972)
Dir. Sidney J. Furie

THE LAST SAMURAI (2003)
Dir. Edward Zwick

LOST IN TRANSLATION (2003)
Dir. Sofia Coppola

THE LOVERS ON THE BRIDGE (1991)
Dir. Leos Carax

OCEAN'S ELEVEN (2001)
Dir. Steven Soderbergh

OPENING NIGHT (1977)
Dir. John Cassavetes

OTHELLO (1952)
Dir. Orson Welles

TRUTH

OTHELLO (1995)
Dir. Oliver Parker

MAGNOLIA (1999)
Dir. Paul Thomas Anderson

MARY (2005)
Dir. Abel Ferrara

MIDNIGHT COWBOY (1969)
Dir. John Schlesinger

MONSTER (2003)
Dir. Patty Jenkins

MONSTER'S BALL (2001)
Dir. Marc Forster

NASHVILLE (1975)
Dir. Robert Altman

ONE FLEW OVER THE CUCKOO'S NEST
(1975) Dir. Milos Forman

PAPER MOON (1973)
Dir. Peter Bogdanovich

PRETTY WOMAN (1990)
Dir. Garry Marshall

PULP FICTION (1994)
Dir. Quentin Tarantino

RAGING BULL (1980)
Dir. Martin Scorsese

REQUIEM FOR A DREAM (2000)
Dir. Darren Aronofsky

SUSAN BATSON

SCARAMOUCH (1952)
Dir. George Sidney

THE SEARCHERS (1956)
Dir. John Ford

THE SIXTH SENSE (1999)
Dir. M. Night Shyamalan

SLEEPLESS IN SEATTLE (1993)
Dir. Nora Ephron

SWEET AND LOWDOWN (1999)
Dir. Woody Allen

TAXI DRIVER (1976)
Dir. Martin Scorsese

TRAFFIC (2000)
Dir. Steven Soderbergh

TRAINING DAY (2001)
Dir. Antoine Fuqua

WHAT'S LOVE GOT TO DO WITH IT (1993)
Dir. Brian Gibson

THE WILD BUNCH (1969)
Dir. Sam Peckinpah

A WOMAN UNDER THE INFLUENCE (1974)
Dir. John Cassavetes

WUTHERING HEIGHTS (1939)
Dir. William Wyler

CPSIA information can be obtained
at www.ICGtesting.com
Printed in the USA
LVHW021815200720
661149LV00019B/1619